A CITIZEN LOOKS AT CONGRESS

books by DEAN ACHESON

A Democrat Looks at His Party
A Citizen Looks at Congress

DEAN ACHESON

A CITIZEN LOOKS AT CONGRESS

HARPER & BROTHERS NEW YORK

Library of Congress catalog card number: 57-6124

CONTENTS

ACKNOWLEDGMENTS

It is a pleasant obligation to express my gratitude to the University of Virginia for its invitation to inaugurate the Edward R. Stettinius, Jr., Memorial Lectures, which stimulated me to the work resulting in this volume; to the *Yale Review*, which published one of its chapters in the Summer Issue, 1956; to Mr. Sidney Hyman, who read the manuscript and out of his wealth of knowledge of the American Presidency made a host of helpful suggestions; and to Miss Barbara Evans, whose contributions of thought and material have enriched the content and whose editing and criticism have lessened the error between these covers.

A CITIZEN LOOKS AT CONGRESS

INTRODUCTION

In 1883 a young man closed his law office in Atlanta, Georgia, and with it his legal career. Neither office nor career was yet a year old. It seems unlikely that the bar suffered from this early repudiation of it. For the young man had little taste for the law. Already he was complaining of "the dreadful drudgery which attends the initiation into our profession." [1] Certainly both the man and his country were to profit greatly from the new start.

The Atlanta bar was abandoned in favor of the classrooms and library of the Johns Hopkins University in Baltimore. Johns Hopkins, still in its first decade, was the center of the most exhilarating intellectual life and educational development in the United States. Its first president, Daniel Coit Gilman, then at the height of his powers, has remained,

[1] Ray Stannard Baker, *Woodrow Wilson, Life and Letters— Youth 1856-1890* (Doubleday, Page & Co., Garden City, 1927), p. 152.

with Charles W. Eliot of Harvard, at the pinnacle of American university presidents. In an atmosphere invigorated by the infusion of German ideas of scholarship and research, the ex-lawyer, denied a scholarship, pursued "special studies in history and political science." [2] It was, he wrote, "the best place in America to study." [3]

His ideas on these subjects had, under the influence of Bagehot, acquired a definite bent,[4] but were not yet crystallized. Somewhat like his views about his name, they were forming but not fully formed. He had tried "a series of experiments with Thos. W., T. Woodrow and plain T." Wilson. At a slightly earlier date he had practiced writing the signature, "Thomas Woodrow Wilson, Senator from Virginia." [5]

The years at Johns Hopkins were years of hard work, intense and shrewd observation, intellectual development and discipline. Wilson's work and interest centered in the seminar conducted by Dr. Herbert B. Adams. At first the student chafed at what he regarded as the rigidity of his prescribed

[2] *Ibid.*, p. 171.

[3] *Ibid.*, p. 173.

[4] See "Cabinet Government in the United States," *International Review*, August, 1879.

[5] David Loth, *The Story of Woodrow Wilson* (The Woodrow Wilson Foundation, New York, 1955), pp. 8, 7.

work. Taking his courage in his hands, he went to
Dr. Adams asking permission to strike out on a
plan of study and writing of his own. To his sur-
prise the door he expected to have to batter down
was gladly opened for him. His plan would have
been an ambitious one for a mature and experienced
scholar. "It is my purpose," he wrote to his fiancée,
"to show, as well as I can, our constitutional system
as it looks in operation." [6] "An immense literature
has already accumulated upon this subject;" he went
on, "but I venture to think that the greater part of
it is either irrelevant or already antiquated." [7] One
bows in respectful admiration before such courage
and confidence.

The confidence was justified. The work went on
in 1883 and 1884, with Wilson writing out in long-
hand, revising, and then copying on his typewriter
chapter after chapter. Each chapter was brought to
the seminar to be read aloud and then debated and
criticized by his teacher and fellow students. As
the months passed, awareness of the quality of
Wilson's work grew. An entry in the record of the
seminar reads: "The principal paper of the evening
was by Mr. Wilson. . . . Mr. Wilson's work is bet-

[6] Baker, *Woodrow Wilson, Life and Letters,* p. 213.
[7] *Ibid.,* p. 214.

ter than anything . . . that has been done hereto-
fore in the Seminary." [8] As in all creative work, its
author had his moments of revulsion and depression,
moments when he wrote of "sentences of which I
am now so tired . . . the style which is so disgust-
ing to me . . . I am comforting myself, as Lysias
did, with the reflection that others into whose hands
these essays come will probably read them only once
and so escape the contempt bred by familiarity." [9]

In 1884 the work was finished and sent off to a
publisher. Days of anxious waiting followed, all
forgotten when the note of acceptance came. The
book appeared in 1885 and was immediately hailed
in words which left no doubt of its success. Gamaliel
Bradford wrote in *The Nation* of February 12, 1885,
"We have no hesitation in saying that this is one
of the most important books, dealing with political
subjects, which have ever issued from the American
press." [10] In the next fifteen years it went through
fifteen editions.

One who reads the book seventy years later
comes to the same conclusion as Bradford. It is a
most important and penetrating book. And yet over
it hangs an atmosphere of melancholy and of irony.

[8] *Ibid.*, p. 219.
[9] *Ibid.*, p. 215.
[10] *Ibid.*, p. 223.

Of melancholy, because, as Wilson's biographer says, "In the end, it is scarcely too much to say, he fell a victim to the defects [in the constitutional structure] he had so clearly perceived." [11] Of irony, because one of the central themes, the decline of the Presidency, was to be conclusively disproved by Woodrow Wilson, twenty-eighth President of the United States.

The theme of the book is that Congress is the central and predominant power in our governmental system and a discussion of what is necessary, in the author's judgment, to make that power fully effective and responsible.

The argument may be briefly outlined. In practice "the literary theory" of the Constitution had broken down. "While we have been shielding it from criticism it has slipped away from us." [12] This was a theory of checks and balances—of which John Adams found eight in writing to John Tyler. Chiefly they were the balance of the state governments and the people against the federal government; and, within the latter, the separation and mutual checks of the legislative, executive, and judicial powers. But out

[11] *Ibid.*, p. 227.

[12] Woodrow Wilson, *Congressional Government* (Houghton Mifflin Company, The Riverside Press, Cambridge, 15th Edition), p. 6.

of a century of developing a continent and out of a civil war, the federal had emerged, visible to every citizen, as "the greater and more sovereign power." [13] The doctrine of implied powers under the Constitution was the legal instrument of this achievement. Within the federal government the judicial power ceased to be a real check and balance to the legislature once it had "declared itself without authority to question the legislature's privilege of determining the nature and extent of its own powers in the choice of means for giving effect to its constitutional prerogatives." [14] And that other theoretical check, the executive, had proved ineffective because the power of the Presidency had waned, "fallen from its first estate of dignity" [15] in the early days of the Republic, as the power of Congress in the test of action became predominant.

The bulk of the book, and its abiding value, is an analysis and description of Congress and its opera-

[13] *Ibid.*, p. 26.

[14] *Ibid.*, pp. 23-24. "But where the law is not prohibited, and is really calculated to effect any of the objects intrusted to the government, to undertake here to inquire into the degree of its necessity, would be to pass the line which circumscribes the judicial department, and to tread on legislative ground. This court disclaims all pretensions to such a power." Marshall, C. J., in *McCulloch v. Maryland*, 4 Wheaton 315, 422 (1819).

[15] Wilson, *Congressional Government*, p. 43.

tion. Here the weakness discerned was in leadership and responsibility, because in practice both had been diffused through the committee system. The young author found the path of progress in the direction of the parliamentary system where authority, party leadership, and responsibility for governmental action might be joined. As the years went by, he was to come to a different conclusion.

I

THE CONGRESS

The Committee System—The Diffusion of Power

At the very outset of his analysis Wilson put his finger upon the central factor in the development of congressional power, the factor of method and organization.

In the first years of the Republic, Congress "not having as yet learned the art of governing itself . . . was glad to get guidance and suggestions of policy from the Executive." [1] But very soon this was changed as Congress organized itself for action. "It very early divided itself into standing committees which it equipped with very comprehensive and thorough-going privileges of legislative initiative and control, and set itself through these to administer the government. Congress is (to adopt Mr. Bagehot's description of Parliament) 'nothing less than a big meeting of more or less idle people. In

[1] Wilson, *Congressional Government*, p. 44.

proportion as you give it power it will inquire into everything, settle everything, meddle in everything. In an ordinary despotism the powers of the despot are limited by his bodily capacity, and by the calls of pleasure; he is but one man; there are but twelve hours in his day, and he is not disposed to employ more than a small part in dull business: he keeps the rest for the court, or the harem, or for society.' But Congress 'is a despot who has unlimited time,— who has unlimited vanity,—who has, or believes he has, unlimited comprehension,—whose pleasure is in action, whose life is work.' " [2]

In Wilson's view, "unquestionably, the predominant and controlling force, the centre and source of all motive and of all regulative power, is Congress." [3] And, even more specifically, he insisted "that it is now, though a wide departure from the form of things, 'no great departure from the fact' to describe ours as a government by the Standing Committees of Congress." [4] The standing committees were the focus of congressional power and the means of its exercise. It was this which gave it its unique characteristics, reflected both in the nature

[2] *Ibid.*, pp. 44-45.
[3] *Ibid.*, p. 11.
[4] *Ibid.*, p. 56.

of congressional leadership and of congressional policy.

At the outset Wilson notes two facts so obvious and familiar that their deep significance and profound effect are often missed. One is that the number of the committees is legion; indeed, "there are as many Standing Committees as there are leading classes of legislation." [5] The second fact is that these committees are bipartisan in composition. They are not working instruments of the majority party. Both majority and minority are represented on them, and the numbers from each party are nearly equal. It takes a very considerable disparity in party membership in the Senate for the majority on a committee to be greater than one, and in the House, with one exception, for it to be greater than two to five.

From these facts grow consequences. "The leaders of the House [and, we may add, of the Senate too] are the chairmen of the principal Standing Commit-

[5] *Ibid.*, p. 60. In the Preface to the Fifteenth Edition (p. vi) Wilson wrote in 1900: "The number of committees in both Senate and House is constantly on the increase. It is now usually quite sixty in the House, and in the Senate more than forty." Despite the LaFollette-Monroney Act of 1946, the standing committees, subcommittees, and joint committees of the two Houses increased from 216 in 1945 to 231 in 1955. *New York Times,* Nov. 21, 1955, p. 17.

tees. Indeed, to be exactly accurate, the House has
as many leaders as there are subjects of legislation." [6]
"It is this multiplicity of leaders, this many-headed
leadership, which makes the organization of the
House too complex to afford uninformed people
and unskilled observers any easy clue to its methods
of rule. For the chairmen of the Standing Committees do not constitute a coöperative body like a
ministry. They do not consult and concur in the
adoption of homogeneous and mutually helpful
measures; . . . Each Committee goes its own way
at its own pace." [7]

To be sure, the Speaker is "a great party chief," [8]
but he is not *the* leader. The Rules Committee has
great power, and, in a later day, the informal Steer-
ing Committee, like the Policy Committees in the
Senate, is not without effect; but at bottom the
committees and their chairmen, potent through experience and seniority, shape, control, and present
legislation. In the last confusing hours of a session the two chairmen and a handful of members
of both parties, comprising the conference committee between the Houses, may write the most
important provisions. But these men, powerful as

[6] Wilson, *Congressional Government*, p. 60.
[7] *Ibid.*, p. 61.
[8] *Ibid.*, p. 60.

they are in Congress, are little known outside of it, which led Wilson to observe that "though the Committees lead in legislation, they lead without concert or responsibility, and lead nobody in particular." [9]

The second fact, the bipartisan composition of the committees, also has its consequences. "It is plainly," wrote Wilson, "the representation of both parties on the Committees that makes party responsibility indistinct and organized party action almost impossible. If the Committees were composed entirely of members of the majority, and were thus constituted representatives of the party in power, the whole course of congressional proceedings would unquestionably take on a very different aspect. There would then certainly be a compact opposition to face the organized majority. Committee reports would be taken to represent the views of the party in power." "It may be said, therefore," he continues, "that very few of the measures which come before Congress are party measures. . . . Indeed, only a very slight examination of the measures which originate with the Committees is necessary to show that most of them are framed with a view to securing their easy passage by giving them as neutral and inoffensive a character as possible.

[9] *Ibid.*, pp. 185-186.

The manifest object is to dress them to the liking of all factions.

"Under such circumstances, neither the failure nor the success of any policy inaugurated by one of the Committees can fairly be charged to the account of either party." [10]

Time has modified to some extent, but has not invalidated, these observations. As we shall see, the rebirth of presidential prestige, the development by the administration in power of programs of "must" legislation, and the direct communication which the radio and television make possible between the President and the voters are all new factors since 1885. But students of the doctrine and the demand for bipartisanship in the politics of our day will find one of its deepest roots in the historic bipartisan composition of the standing committees, which are the ultimate repositories of congressional power.

As I have suggested, the preponderance of the majority party on the committees is for the most part small. The vagaries of attendance and the shift of a few votes can easily change the outcome. But more important still is the fact that each of these committees tends to develop a life of its own, in which members hold individual, rather than strictly

[10] *Ibid.,* pp. 99-101.

party, attitudes and where the influence of strong
and set characters is great. For instance, the attitude
of Senator Millikin of Colorado toward reciprocal
trade legislation in the Finance Committee, or of
Representative Reed of New York on a tax measure
in the Ways and Means Committee, was more likely
to influence than to be influenced by the views of
others, including a President of their own party.

The heart and center of the legislative process,
the redoubt of congressional power, lies in these
committees, controlled, in Wilson's phrase, by "the
elders of the assembly," [11] who, by reason of the independence gained by their proven strength in
their constituencies and flowing also from the near
balance of parties and the peculiar corporate life
in the committees, are well insulated from party
discipline. They control the content, form, timing,
and appearance or nonappearance of legislation. The
ambitious and eager new member soon learns that
"as a rule, a bill committed is a bill doomed. When
it goes from the clerk's desk to a committee-room
it crosses a parliamentary bridge of sighs to dim
dungeons of silence whence it will never return." [12]

True as this observation remains today as to
what we might call members' private bills, it is no

[11] *Ibid.*, p. 102.
[12] *Ibid.*, p. 69.

longer a wholly accurate description of the committees' powers toward major administration measures. For such a bill the "dim dungeons of silence" still exist to which *lettres de cachet* may consign bills, but not for life. They can be, and are, produced before the bar of Congress—often haggard and transformed by their imprisonment—by a presidential *habeas corpus*; if the demand is made often enough and vigorously enough.

In the years since Wilson wrote—and in no small measure due to the influence of President Wilson himself—an important change has come about in the roles played by the President and the Congress in the enactment of major legislation. In stating this change in a sentence, one is apt to overstate it. I, perhaps, do so in saying that Wilson described a relationship in which Congress initiated and formulated legislation and the President approved or vetoed it: while, today, in the field of major administration measures, the President initiates and formulates legislation; the Congress modifies, approves, or vetoes. This change has come about through the sheer necessity in today's world for an interrelated and coherent legislative program, and the recognition of this necessity by strong Presidents. The very nature of congressional leadership, its many-headed-ness, and the bipartisan composition of the committees prevented that leadership, alone and unaided, from putting through homogeneous and interrelated measures. For there was no controllable and controlling party organization to plan and produce them. "The legislation of a session [did] not represent the policy of either [the majority or minority]; it [was] simply an aggregate of the bills recommended by Committees composed of members from both sides of the House, and it [was] known to be usually, not the work of the majority men upon the Committees, but compromise conclusions bearing some shade or tinge of each of the variously-colored opinions and wishes of the committee-men of both parties." [13]

As Wilson saw it, the Senate "has those same radical defects of organization which weaken the House. Its functions also, like those of the House, are segregated in the prerogatives of numerous Standing Committees. In this regard Congress is all of a piece. . . . Its proceedings bear most of the characteristic features of committee rule. Its conclusions are suggested now by one set of its members, now by another set, and again by a third; . . . Some Senators are, indeed, seen to be of larger men-

[13] *Ibid.*, p. 99.

tal stature and built of stauncher moral stuff than
their fellow-members. . . . But such a man, however eminent, is never more than *a* Senator. No one
is *the* Senator. No one may speak for his party as
well as for himself; no one exercises the special trust
of acknowledged leadership . . . the weight of
every criticism uttered in its chamber depends upon
the weight of the critic who utters it, deriving little if
any addition to its specific gravity from connection
with the designs of a purposeful party organization.
I cannot insist too much upon this defect of congressional government, because it is evidently radical. Leadership with authority over a great ruling
party is a prize to attract great competitors, and is
in a free government the only prize that will attract
great competitors." [14]

It was, perhaps, in the area of revenue and supply
that congressional government reached the peak
of incoherence and confusion, illustrating again the
truth that "the more power is divided the more irresponsible it becomes." [15] In 1884, said Wilson, "The
national income is controlled by one Committee of
of the House and one of the Senate; the expenditures of the government are regulated by fifteen
Committees of the House and five of the Senate;

[14] *Ibid.*, pp. 212-214.
[15] *Ibid.*, p. 93.

and the currency is cared for by two Committees of the House and one of the Senate." [16] "No other nation on earth," said a writer in the *New York Nation* on November 30, 1882, "attempts such a thing, or could attempt it without soon coming to grief, our salvation thus far consisting in an enormous income, with practically no drain for military expenditure." [17] The latter half of our basis for salvation is gone, yet the confusion remains and is only lessened in so far as the executive can insist that the two sides of the ledger, income and outgo, be considered and planned together. The growth of the executive budget, beginning in the Presidencies of Taft and Wilson and greatly developed in the past twenty years, has been an important element in the growth of presidential authority.

In 1946 Congress made a gallant attempt to reform itself. Section 138 of the Legislative Reorganization Act of 1946 provided that the Committees on Ways and Means of the House, on Finance of the Senate, and on Appropriations of both Houses should meet jointly at the beginning of each regular session and report a resolution estimating the revenues for the next fiscal year and fixing the maximum amount which might be appropriated. If it should

[16] *Ibid.*, p. 136.
[17] *Ibid.*, p. 191.

appear that outgo was not to be met by income,
the law required that the resolution must recite the
distasteful conclusion, "That it is the sense of
the Congress that the public debt shall be increased." [18] After one horrendous and exhausting
attempt to follow this procedure in 1947, the
section by common and tacit consent was ig-
nored, and Congress reverted to the old system by
which revenue was considered and planned by the
Ways and Means Committee of the House and the
Finance Committee of the Senate, while the authorization of expenditures was considered by innumerable standing committees; appropriations, by
the Appropriations Committees of the two Houses;
and the public debt and currency, by the two Bank-
ing and Currency Committees. In a true sense, then,
the actual federal budget is not a plan but a result,
and can only be known when the session of Congress
is over.

Throughout young Mr. Wilson's analysis ran
some assumptions which, perhaps, seemed more
obvious in 1884 than they do today. On nearly every
page we see his impatience with the lack of neat-
ness in congressional organization and his belief
that it is both possible and desirable for the legislative process in Congress to be organized into a

[18] 79th Cong., 2d Sess., 60 Stat. 812, 832-833.

contest between compact and disciplined parties—
majority and opposition. This, he contends, would
sharpen differences, bring home responsibility for
action taken, and give the electorate clear-cut
choices. So method, mechanics in government, seems
to him of very great importance. "The most striking
contrast in modern politics," he writes, "is not between presidential and monarchical governments,
but between Congressional and Parliamentary governments." [19]

To us in the middle of the twentieth century that
contrast does not seem the most striking in modern
politics. Far more striking and fundamental is to us
the contrast between democratic government and
totalitarian government. The difference transcends
method and goes to the basic values and ends
which governments pursue. We have learned, too,
that democratic government in a free society is
possible—certainly is successful—only when the
parties which compete for the support of the voters
and the control of the government believe and act
upon the presuppositions and restraints of the free
society. The system will not work if a substantial
group uses the machinery of the system to destroy
it. But even short of this, democratic government
works best when the relations and fortunes of large

[19] Wilson, *Congressional Government*, pp. xv-xvi.

groups are not suddenly and drastically impaired by a change in the control of government. For changes of this sort strike at one of the conditions which make democratic government possible—that it be government by consent, not coercion, and that the consent include the consent of those in control of government to surrender control when, under the system, the popular will so directs.

The tradition of permitting a fair ascertainment of the popular will and readily accepting it is strong, but it would be strained if a change in control meant persecution of the defeated by the victors or a drastic change in the social order. Certainly one can see grave problems arising if, say, one party, being successful, would put into effect a broad program of nationalization and the other, if successful, of denationalization. After industries had been nationalized two or three times, denationalization would be impossible. There would be no investors willing to accept such hazards. So the issue would be resolved by a sort of Gresham's law; the willingness to let the system operate freely would be severely strained.

The sharpening of issues accompanied by a tightening of party discipline can easily lead, as Sidney Hyman has pointed out, to a series of purges by which the less extreme and zealous partisans are eliminated. This makes for an increasing ideological basis for party membership, an increase in dogmatism on one side forcing an increase on the other. The end is likely to be the collapse of one of the parties in an electoral disaster or the fragmentation of both, a reproduction of the French political scene. Neither result is favorable to the success of democratic government. In the United States, with its continental sweep and sectional distinctions, it is useful and important that each party shall have in it some element of the other to voice the sentiments of interests which, through changes of government, have lost a more dominant influence. There is much wisdom in Denis Brogan's observation:

in a vast country, of continental range and variety, with sectional interests, traditions, passions to be allowed for, a highly integrated and responsible party system might mean the imposition, by a numerical majority, of its views and interests and passions on great minorities, spread over great territorial areas, creating in those regions a sense of outrage dearly bought by a symmetrical party programme. Such a sectional party triumph and such a sectional party programme brought about the Civil War.[20]

[20] D. W. Brogan, *Politics in America* (Harper & Brothers, New York, 1954), p. 90.

This is not a plea for intra-party factions as a positive good. Obviously it is harmful when a substantial segment of the party leads a revolt against presidential leadership, as was done when President Truman's vetoes of the Internal Security Act of 1950 and the McCarran-Walter Immigration Act were overridden. The orderly development of wise national policies was impeded. But Wilson was wrong, I think, in laying so much stress on the element of party discipline in producing strong government. More room is needed for flexibility than he allowed. Not the least of its utilities is in permitting the President to gain support across party lines for policies which need continuity for long periods, without opening those of the opposition who support him to the charge of apostasy.

The Extension of Congressional Control
of Administration

The Constitution gives only the broadest sort of guidance as to what comprises "legislative" power and what "executive" power. "The separation of the powers of government did not make each branch completely autonomous. It left each, in some measure, dependent upon the others, as it left to each

power to exercise, in some respects, functions in
their nature executive, legislative and judicial." [21]
So, when it is said that the legislature has en-
croached on the executive prerogative, or vice versa,
it should be understood that this is usually a polem-
ical statement expressing condemnation of what is
believed to be undesirable practice in the fluid and
changing interplay of forces in our political life.
The least useful—and the most common—way of
discussing legislative-executive friction is to quote
extracts from the constitutional opinions of the Supreme Court. Over a century ago de Tocqueville
pointed out this national characteristic of ours:
"Scarcely any political question arises in the United
States that is not resolved, sooner or later, into a
judicial question." [22] It is a political question, which
cannot be answered by court citations, how much
discretion should be delegated by the Congress
and to what extent the Congress should attempt to
supervise and control its administration. It is a
political question, where both legislative and executive have power to initiate the use of military action

[21] Mr. Justice Brandeis, dissenting, in *Myers v. United States,*
272 U.S. 52, 291 (1926).

[22] Alexis de Tocqueville, *Democracy in America* (Alfred A.
Knopf, New York, 1945), Vol. I, p. 280.

in support of American interests, which should wait for the other to act—a political question which may vary greatly with particular circumstances.

The Constitution, in defining the President's duties, declares that "he shall take Care that the Laws be faithfully executed." [23] This is clearly an executive function. Indeed the control and supervision of administration are the heart of that function. But it is also clear that the Congress has an equally proper interest in watching, investigating, and criticizing the administration of the laws it enacts. For almost a hundred years Congress has increasingly been moving into this field of endeavor, and there was bound to be some jostling. But it is an error to think of it only as a competitive struggle between the legislature and the executive with the attempt to encroach, on the one hand, and to resist encroachment, on the other. The interplay is broader than this. Each does its utmost to influence, often to compel, the other; and so vague is the division between the powers that each can insist upon the legitimacy of what it does.

The method by which Congress gained the capacity to supervise and control administration lay in a master stroke of organization, the division into stand-

[23] Constitution of the United States, Art. II, Sec. 3.

ing committees, each with its task and jurisdiction.
The vast energy which this division of labor re-
leased has to be experienced to be believed. More
than 200 standing, sub-, and joint committees,
staffed by approximately a thousand employed per-
sonnel and drawing on the energies of 435 Members
of Congress and 96 Senators, can develop attack in
breadth or defense in depth, or both at the same
time. Not only can, but do.

"Each standing committee," says the Legislative
Reorganization Act of 1946 (and it merely stated
the practice of years), ". . . shall exercise continuous watchfulness of the execution by the administrative agencies concerned of any laws, the subject matter of which is within the jurisdiction of such
committee." [24]

Besides the substantive standing committees each
House has had for decades a Committee on Expenditures in the Executive Departments, now
known as the Committee on Government Operations, of which we have heard a good deal lately.[25]
Among its duties is "studying the operation of Gov-

---

[24] 79th Cong., 2d Sess., 60 Stat. 812, 832.

[25] The name was changed in the Senate by Sen. Res. 280,
82d Cong., 2d Sess., March 3, 1952; and in the House by
H. Res. 647, July 3, 1952.

ernment activities at all levels with a view to determining its economy and efficiency." [26] This lends
assurance that nothing will be overlooked and a
good deal will be double checked.

How this "continuous watchfulness" merges into
control is shown by the annual appropriations acts
for the executive departments and agencies. Here
the word "continuous" is particularly apt. The appropriations acts are usually enacted into law in late
June. By that time the departmental staffs are already at work upon next year's requests which will
come before the subcommittees of the Appropriations Committees when Congress convenes in January. For this purpose, subcommittees are established.[27] Their power, due to the vastness of the
undertaking, is great. And the vastness of the undertaking is due to the practice, inaugurated by
Congress in 1862, of detailed appropriations, "mi-
nutely specifying the uses to be made of the funds
appropriated." "In this, as in other things," wrote
Wilson, "the appetite for government on the part
of Congress has grown with that perfection of

[26] Legislative Reorganization Act of 1946, 79th Cong., 2d
Sess., 60 Stat. 812, 816, 825.

[27] In the Second Session of the 84th Congress the size of the
subcommittees of the House committee ranged from five to
thirteen members; and of the Senate committee, from five to
fifteen members.

organization which has rendered the gratification of its desire for power easily attainable." [28] Each head of an office or suboffice in a department appears before the subcommittee to justify what he and his subordinates do, or don't do, why they do it, and how. This leads directly into the details of administration, such as electronic equipment of the Voice of America and its location, the desirability and efficacy of its programs, the selection of paintings or plays to be sponsored for production abroad, the military plans of NATO, and so on, to speak of the foreign field only. It involves extended debate on matters of policy—should more or less money or none be spent on programs which involve Tito, or India, or Franco, or Chiang Kai-shek, and are the policies well or ill conceived? The competence and views of individual officers may be raised, particularly if they work in a field currently the subject of controversy, such as the Information Service or the Far East.

Further complication is introduced by the fact that appropriations do not involve only the Appropriations Committees. Under the rules of the two Houses no appropriation shall be reported in any general appropriation bill, or be in order as an amendment, for any expenditure not previously

[28] Wilson, *Congressional Government*, p. 151.

authorized by law.[29] These simple words have the
deepest significance in legislative method. They
mean that, before the Appropriations Committees
and the Congress will grant money for any purpose,
a prior bill, authorizing the activity to be financed,
must be considered by different committees in the
two Houses and enacted by the Congress. When to
this is added the practice, which has become common during and since the war, of requiring annual
authorization acts as well as appropriations acts,
the power of Congress over administration becomes
great indeed.

A glance at two instances will show how great.
During the war, the lend-lease program, and after
the war, the Marshall Plan and the succeeding
technical and military assistance programs required annually four separate and detailed reviews
before four separate congressional committees, the
Foreign Affairs Committee of the House, the Foreign Relations Committee of the Senate, and the
two Appropriations Committees. The function of
the first two committees was to report bills authorizing continuance of the programs for another
year and to fix the maximum amount which could
be appropriated; that of the second two commit-

[29] House Rule XXI, Sec. 2; Senate Rule XVI, Sec. 1.

tees, to appropriate in detail. By the time one year's work was over, it was time to begin on the next. Some officers of the agencies did nothing else and the amount of time and energy of all officials which went into the new task of keeping the program alive and solvent was enormous. There was, of course, the inevitable necessity for each committee to find some items to be cut. But the chief result was to reduce the area of administrative flexibility in work which demanded a high degree of flexibility.

Provisions were written into the law, pretty well delimiting the type of program which could be put into effect, about the use of American shipping, about undertakings which recipient governments must make. Informal understandings were reached about allocations of funds among countries. Illustrative programs, intended to justify typical needs, tended to become required programs. The organization and location of authority over the administrative staff at home and abroad became, particularly after the war, of absorbing interest to Congress. One reorganization followed another, with the role of the Department of State the chief source of controversy and of confusion, not without cost to the conduct of our foreign relations. Starting as an executive agency independent of and separate from the State Department, the administrative staff has now been covered into that department, but still on a semi-autonomous basis.

Nor does the machinery of congressional supervision end with the process of authorizing and making appropriations. The "watchdog" or special committee bears a modern name but derives from the Committee on the Conduct and Expenditures of the War, of Civil War fame, and the more recent Truman Committee of the Second World War. The Economic Cooperation Act of 1948 (Marshall Plan Act) provided for a Joint Committee on Foreign Economic Cooperation of ten members and its own staff "to make a continuous study of the programs of United States economic assistance to foreign countries. . . . The Administrator, at the request of the committee, shall consult with the committee from time to time with respect to his activities under this Act." [30] One begins to appreciate—as the executive agencies certainly do—how far from alone the President is in performing his

[30] 80th Cong., 2d Sess., 62 Stat. 137, 156. In accordance with congressional practice, it was made up of six majority members and four minority members. Its membership was made up of three members each from the Senate Foreign Relations Committee and the House Foreign Affairs Committee, and two members from each of the two Appropriations Committees, appointed by the respective chairmen of those committees.

constitutional duty of taking "Care that the Laws be faithfully executed."

Nor have I yet exhausted the catalogue of congressional resources. There remains the investigatory power of Congress. Some investigations are the necessary prelude to legislation. And "Legislation," observed Wilson, "unquestionably generates legislation. . . . Every statute in its turn has a numerous progeny. . . . Once begin the dance of legislation, and you must struggle through its mazes as best you can to its breathless end,—if any end there be." [31] So there are as many subjects for study as there are bills which can be written. But the investigatory power is broader than this.

The Congress has the right "to look diligently into every affair of government and to talk much about what it sees." It may acquaint "itself with the acts and the disposition of the administrative agents of the government," [32] so that the country may know how it is being served. It may inquire into the state of affairs in every branch of our national life, including such seemingly unlikely fields for federal action as local gambling and crime; for who knows where something may turn up which may involve federal office holders or the national welfare? But

[31] Wilson, *Congressional Government*, p. 297.
[32] *Ibid.*, p. 303.

the happiest hunting ground is investigation into administration. For, as we have seen, the urge in Congress to supervise and control administration is very great.

Legislation, by itself and without more, induces an element of frustration. It is all well enough to issue commands; but the sense of power and accomplishment is denied when one cannot direct the execution, holding its human instruments to strict accountability and dismissing them when their performance is unsatisfactory. To the young Wilson of 1884 it seemed self-evident "that the representatives of the people are the proper ultimate authority in all matters of government, and that administration is merely the clerical part of government. Legislation is the originating force. It determines what shall be done." [33] And yet, with all its power, Congress cannot quite bend the executive agents to its will. "Once installed, their hold upon their offices does not depend upon the will of Congress." [34] The Secretaries, of whom Wilson had no high opinion at any time, "are denied the gratification of possessing real power, but they have the satisfaction of being secure in a petty independence

[33] *Ibid.*, p. 273.
[34] *Ibid.*, p. 272.

which gives them a chance to be tricky and schem-
ing." [35]

So the frustration continues. "Congress stands
almost helplessly outside of the departments. Even
the special, irksome, ungracious investigations which
it from time to time institutes . . . do not afford it
more than a glimpse of the inside of a small province
of federal administration. . . . It can violently dis-
turb, but it cannot often fathom, the waters of the
sea in which the bigger fish of the civil service swim
and feed. Its dragnet stirs without cleansing the
bottom." [36]

The related powers of investigation and impeach-
ment are tools too heavy and clumsy for the task
of managerial control toward which Congress seems
irresistibly drawn. With these tools, as Wilson put
it, "Congress cannot control the officers of the executive without disgracing them." [37] And the result of
its effort to do so is apt to be a loss of confidence in
both executive and Congress. For Congress "must
draw the public eye by openly avowing a suspicion
of malfeasance, and must then magnify and inten-
sify the scandal by setting its Committees to cross-

[35] *Ibid.*, p. 272.
[36] *Ibid.*, p. 271.
[37] *Ibid.*, p. 278.

examining scared subordinates and sulky ministers. And after all is over and the murder out, probably nothing is done." [38]

In 1884 Wilson saw that what prevented the power of Congress from being supreme, and effectively supreme, was the separation of the legislative and executive powers. "The main purpose," he thought, "of the Convention of 1787 seems to have been to accomplish this grievous mistake. . . . We are in just the case that England was in before she achieved the reform for which we are striving. . . . It was not accomplished until a distinct responsibility of the Ministers of the Crown to one, and to only one, master had been established beyond all uncertainty." [39] But thirty years later he saw the problem in a different light.

[38] *Ibid.*, p. 278.
[39] *Ibid.*, pp. 284-285.

II

THE PRESIDENCY

"The prestige of the presidential office," Wilson wrote in 1884, "has declined with the character of the Presidents. And the character of the Presidents has declined as the perfection of selfish party tactics has advanced." [1] "When the presidential candidate came to be chosen, it was recognized as imperatively necessary that he should have as short a political record as possible, and that he should wear a clean and irreproachable insignificance." [2] "That high office has fallen from its first estate of dignity because its power has waned; and its power has waned because the power of Congress has become predominant." [3] "There is no office set apart for the great party leader in our government . . . the presidency is too silent and inactive, too little

[1] Wilson, *Congressional Government*, p. 42.
[2] *Ibid.*, p. 42.
[3] *Ibid.*, p. 43.

like a premiership and too much like a superintendency." [4] "[Except for his veto power] the President
might, not inconveniently, be a permanent officer;
the first official of a carefully-graded and impartially
regulated civil service system, through whose sure
series of merit-promotions the youngest clerk might
rise even to the chief magistracy." [5]

Wilson was eight years old when the guns fell
silent at Appomattox and Lincoln was laid in his
grave. Writing in 1884, he had grown up in the
Presidencies of Johnson, Grant, Hayes, Garfield, and
Arthur, Presidencies which his book described, as it
described those from Jackson's to the war years.
Nevertheless, it is in the discussion of the Presidency that the youth and the theoretical, even mech-
anistic, approach of the author are most evident.
One misses the broader setting in the society of
which the government structure he discusses is a
part and in the still greater world of which that
society, in turn, is a part. Congress and President
are seen as actors on a stage cut off and confined
by the footlights of his scrutiny and the scenery
of Capitol Hill.

"There is here," Sidney Hyman writes to me,
"little sense of the historic ebb and flow in con-

[4] *Ibid.*, pp. 203-204.
[5] *Ibid.*, p. 254.

gressional-executive relations; of how Jefferson, though speaking of the Congress as 'the generating organ of the people' and of the President as merely the administrative agent for the 'objects and situations' defined by the Congress, nevertheless invisibly ruled the Congress by his rule of the dominant political party of the time; of how Jefferson, again, in his indirect but firm assertion of presidential leadership was followed by 'King Caucus'; of how Jackson was followed by seven presidential dwarfs,[6] each hobbled by a Congress that could not make up its own mind about the issues of the day; and how the seven dwarfs, in turn, were followed by Lincoln."

In one respect, however, Wilson, a little later, was to see the relation between the shape of our government and the environment in which it moves and acts.

It is the external world and our relations with it out of which grow the greatness and power of the presidential office. Leadership in our relations with other nations—including that most acute and critical of all relations, war—is by the Constitution entrusted

---

[6] The description is unfair to Polk. Mr. Gerald Johnson has already properly corrected me for classing him among the "minuscule Democrats" (his phrase) in A Democrat Looks at His Party. I do not wish to offend twice.

to the President. When problems of international relations, of war and defense (including civil war), are in the forefront, the power of the Presidency is evoked, its eminence plain enough. In the decades when America was concerned with itself, with the occupation of the continent, with growth and development, the Presidency could understandably be thought "too silent and inactive, too little like a premiership and too much like a superintendency." There is perhaps a double irony in Wilson's remark on the eve of his assuming the office of President of the United States: "It would be the irony of fate if my administration had to deal chiefly with foreign affairs." [7]

Fifteen years after the book was published Wilson corrected his views about the Presidency in the Preface to the Fifteenth Edition. In the intervening years Grover Cleveland had reasserted the President's authority over the conduct of foreign affairs, and the war with Spain had again brought presidential authority to the forefront.

"Much the most important change to be noticed," Wilson wrote in Princeton in the summer of 1900, "is the result of the war with Spain upon the lodgment and exercise of power within our federal system: the greatly increased power and opportunity for

[7] Loth, *The Story of Woodrow Wilson*, p. 23.

constructive statesmanship given the President, by
the plunge into international politics and into the
administration of distant dependencies, which has
been that war's most striking and momentous con-
sequence. When foreign affairs play a prominent
part in the politics and policy of a nation, its Executive must of necessity be its guide: must utter every
initial judgment, take every first step of action, supply the information upon which it is to act, suggest
and in large measure control its conduct. The President of the United States is now, as of course, at the
front of affairs, as no president, except Lincoln, has
been since the first quarter of the nineteenth century, when the foreign relations of the new nation
had first to be adjusted. There is no trouble now
about getting the President's speeches printed and
read, every word. Upon his choice, his character,
his experience hang some of the most weighty issues
of the future. The government of dependencies must
be largely in his hands. Interesting things may come
out of the singular change." [8]

Eight years later, after Theodore Roosevelt had
burnished the power of the presidential office to a
brilliant lustre, Wilson wrote with even greater
conviction: "His is the only national voice in affairs.
Let him once win the admiration and confidence

[8] Wilson, *Congressional Government,* pp. xi-xii.

of the country, and no other single force can withstand him, no combination of forces will easily overpower him. His position takes the imagination of the country. He is the representative of no constituency, but of the whole people. When he speaks in his true character, he speaks for no special interest. If he rightly interpret the national thought and boldly insist upon it, he is irresistible; and the country never feels the zest of action so much as when its President is of such insight and calibre." [9]

To the younger man the representatives of the people, to whom properly belongs ultimate authority, were in the Congress; to the older one, the President was also a representative of the people, indeed the only one elected by all the people, the chosen and acknowledged leader whose view must be national in scope and who need not keep a weather eye cocked toward a parochial constituency. To him it was plain that "Leadership with authority over a great ruling party . . . [which] is in a free government the only prize that will attract great competitors" [10] was the Presidency. It attracted him—and he was to achieve it.

The relation between the President and Congress

[9] Woodrow Wilson, *Constitutional Government in the United States* (Columbia University Press, New York, 1908), p. 68.

[10] Wilson, *Congressional Government*, p. 214.

is not one of repose. There is nothing static about the balance of power set up by the Constitution. It is a kinetic equilibrium, the resultant of the counter-thrusts of strong forces. "The doctrine of the separation of powers was adopted by the Convention of 1787, not to promote efficiency but to preclude the exercise of arbitrary power. The purpose was, not to avoid friction, but, by means of the inevitable friction incident to the distribution of the governmental powers among three departments, to save the people from autocracy." [11]

The nature of congressional power we have seen. The President is well armed also; but his weapons differ, as was the custom in gladiatorial combat, from those of the Congress. The latter is the retiarius seeking to entangle opponents in a cast net and to dispatch them with a trident; the President, the dimachaerus with a sword in each hand.

High among the President's resources are the great executive organizations for collecting, analyzing, and focusing knowledge on the vast congeries of situations amid which, and in relation to which, government must act. Congress must always be dependent upon the executive here. There is no substitute for it, as one knows who has been in the flow

[11] Mr. Justice Brandeis, dissenting, in *Myers v. United States*, 272 U.S. 52, 293 (1926).

of the papers and then is cut off from it. There is a story told that Chief Justice Hughes, on being asked what he would say if the Secretary of State should ask his opinion on a matter then very much occupying public attention, replied, "I would ask for an opportunity to go through the papers." While a grasp of the facts does not assure wise decision, an experienced man would hesitate to concur in or oppose action without it. Here knowledge is indeed power.

With these resources of knowledge, with the leadership of the ruling political party, with the direction of the executive branch, and with the chief magistracy of the nation all rolled into one, the President is the outstanding figure in the country. In these days of radio and television he enters every home and is listened to at every fireside. He talks directly to those who elect every Congressman and Senator. In the hands of a man who knows how to use these powers, and has the courage to do so, they are formidable indeed.

It is, I know, fashionable to state that in the seventy years since Wilson wrote there has been so great and steady a growth of presidential power that the constitutional problem of today is the checking of executive aggrandizement. I do not share this view. True, the power, prestige, and—most certainly

—the responsibilities of the Presidency have grown greatly. But the growth of power has not been steady or maintained. Presidential power is great in times of war, national emergency (such as the Depression), or when the sense of danger from abroad is acute. But when a consciousness of security, normalcy, and prosperity (whether well founded or not) dominates, the power of the office, as a means of positive accomplishment, diminishes in competition with the multitudinous and often inconsistent appeals of congressional leaders. Furthermore, any idea that the contestants put into the arena by the Constitution are ill-matched in power and resources is far from the fact. The question, in my judgment, is whether the checking and balancing prescribed by the Constitution is so conducted as to permit a continuity of policy, involving over a period of years the maintenance of distasteful measures. For this is essential if we and our friends are to maintain our position and safety in competition with powers of unmistakable capacity for consistent and sustained effort. I believe that it is possible to do this only if the presidential office is made and maintained strong and resolute.[12]

[12] I have discussed one area where this is particularly necessary in "The Responsibility for Decision in Foreign Policy," *The Yale Review*, September, 1954.

The central question is not whether the Congress should be stronger than the Presidency, or vice versa; but, how the Congress and the Presidency can both be strengthened to do the pressing work that falls to each to do, and to both to do together.

This is not merely the work contemplated by the founders. For instance, in the last three-quarters of a century the rapid industrialization of the country has brought into existence organizations and forces before which the individual is as impotent as a chip on a flooded stream. The state governments are hardly more effective. To control these forces and organizations "in the public interest," under broad principles declared by Congress, administration of a wholly new type has come into existence. "Independent agencies" have been created to carry out the law—"independent," that is, of the President. They have an amalgam of powers, legislative, judicial, and executive. The process began while Wilson was writing in 1883, with the Civil Service Commission, followed in 1887 with the Interstate Commerce Commission; after that the flood. But, understandably, Wilson does not seem to have been aware of what was occurring or what underlay it. Important segments of administration have escaped the President's legal power of control, though the responsibility for what they do, or don't do, may be laid at his door—for want of a better one. But he is not wholly powerless, since through appointment, the prestige of his office, and his position of party chieftain he is able to influence, if not to exert, legal authority. The result has been quite workable, but it may need further improvisation as the President's duties as chief manager of the economy (recognized in the Employment Act of 1946) require prompt and unified action.

Other developments since Wilson's youth have called for still further responses in the governmental art. Need for economic management antedated the Employment Act of 1946. As great economic interests arose and became conscious of their particularized concerns, they acquired organized and authorized voices outside and inside government. Outside, there were farm groups, labor unions, chambers of commerce, and manufacturers' associations. Inside, Secretaries of Agriculture, Labor, and Commerce, each concerned with a particular sector of the national economy for which they acted as public guardians. Since these private interests often collide in society, so they do in their appeals to government. Here, in judging, the President must stand for the general interest and often must summon the national strength to support his stand in these collisions of giants—and perhaps even more when they avoid collision by uniting their demands. In exercising this vast power, he must be ever watchful that his sources of knowledge remain pure, for the urge to buy or shove a way to these sources is very great.

Again, it sometimes seems that ever since the beginning of the First World War we have been living, if not in a perpetual crisis, in swiftly recurring crises. Here, too, governmental practice has responded to the world around it. The statutes are full of provisions that, upon finding this or that situation to exist, the President may proclaim an emergency, necessary powers shall come into being, and legal consequences follow. This is all wise and essential. But it requires the greatest restraint and purity of purpose on the part of the President, as well as watchfulness and understanding on the part of Congress.

It used to be debated whether the constitutional provision that the President shall be Commander-in-Chief of the Armed Forces went so far as to include command in the field. But the discovery of nuclear weapons has ended that argument. By law the President, and only the President, can authorize their use. This is only the beginning of the problems which the possibility of nuclear warfare has posed to the traditional attitudes towards controlling the use of force.

And these problems are, in turn, only part of a still larger one as our nation has become a leading member of groups of nations, more or less closely knit, whose survival may depend on acting together quickly and wisely. It is no longer enough that our governmental system works well enough within the United States. Is it equipped to play a leading and effective role in a grouping larger than the United States? Indeed, are we and the states associated with us—all responsive in varying degrees to popular will—sufficiently flexible in structure and decisive enough in operation to meet the competition of authoritarian power, which, though it also has serious weaknesses and rigidity, can move with secrecy and speed? There are those who doubt that we are, but I refuse to be defeatist. We have in the past shown the capacity to recognize new developments and to act boldly and swiftly to meet them. We have ingenuity and imagination. The problem of the future should not be insoluble. But to solve this problem we shall need leaders of the cast of mind which Wilson found were distinctive of the first stage of our national growth.

"The three stages of national growth," he wrote,

"which preceded the war between the States were each of them creative of a distinct class of political leaders. In the period of erection there were great architects and master-builders; in the period of constitutional interpretation there were, at a distance from the people, great political schoolmen who pondered and expounded the letter of the law, and, nearer the people, great constitutional advocates who cast the doctrines of the schoolmen into policy; and in the period of abolitionist agitation there were great masters of feeling and leaders of public purpose." [13] The problems which arise in equipping ourselves to play a leading and worthy part in close groupings of nations call for "great architects and master-builders." This is no work for "political schoolmen" and "great masters of feeling," who are apt to be more plentiful.

[13] Wilson, *Congressional Government*, pp. 200-201.

III

LEGISLATIVE-EXECUTIVE RELATIONS

The United States has not taken the road of constitutional development which Wilson advocated in 1884. The Congress has not become supreme, swallowed the executive, and created another in the form of a committee of its own leaders. The Presidency has emerged from weakness to regain leadership and restore the balance designed in the Constitution. With this emergence has come friction, of which Justice Brandeis spoke, as the legislature and the executive have rubbed against each other in the operation of a difficult system under considerable pressure.

When one speaks of the executive working with the Congress, one is using shorthand. The center and focus of legislative-executive relations lie in the congressional committees and in the method of their operation. Much as the President and his associates may influence the Congress through direct appeal to the people, the route from planning to action leads through the committees to legislation. For today nearly all programs require funds, authority, and men, which Congress may grant, skimp, or withhold. Legislation is more than the "oil of government"; it is the essential prerequisite of government. And it is in the committees, where Congress is least susceptible to party discipline, that it gives its legislative answer to the policies of the administration.

There is another fact, also, which must not escape us. While each one of these committees and subcommittees is a channel along which influence may flow from the Congress to the executive, it is quite possible for influence to flow in the other direction along the same channels. If it were not so, our government would be almost impossible to operate. To be sure, Congress has its defenses. Unless an executive officer or employee wishes to risk a year of penitential reverie, he had best not use any appropriated funds "to pay for any personal service, advertisement, telegram, telephone, letter, printed or written matter, or other device, intended or designed to influence in any manner a Member of Congress, to favor or oppose, by vote or otherwise, any legislation or appropriation by Congress, whether before or after the introduction of any bill or resolution." [1]

[1] Act of July 11, 1919, 66th Cong., 1st Sess., 41 Stat. 68, *as amended*, U.S.C., Title 18, Sec. 1913.

And, as Wilson pointed out, consultation with the Senate has a tendency to be all one way. "The President really has no voice at all in the conclusions of the Senate with reference to his diplomatic transactions . . . and yet without a voice in the conclusion there is no consultation." "The Senate," he adds, "when it closes its doors, upon going into 'executive session,' closes them upon the President as much as upon the rest of the world." [2] There is truth in this—bitter truth, as President Wilson, lying on his sickbed while the Senate formulated reservations to the League of Nations Covenant, was to experience. But Wilson overstates the isolation of the Hill and the White House from one another, just as he does when he writes, "His [the President's] only power of compelling compliance on the part of the Senate lies in his initiative in negotiation, which affords him a chance to get the country into such scrapes, so pledged in the view of the world to certain courses of action, that the Senate hesitates to bring about the appearance of dishonor which would follow its refusal to ratify the rash promises or to support the indiscreet threats of the Department of State." [3] If, for instance, one studies the interplay of influence between the Department

[2] Wilson, *Congressional Government*, p. 233.
[3] *Ibid.*, pp. 233-234.

and the committees on the Formosa treaty and legislation of 1955, one can see the bearing of this last observation. Nonetheless, one must conclude, I think, that in the evolution of policy comprised in these measures, the Department and the committees each deeply influenced the other.

In the process of communication and mutual effort to influence between the committees and the executive a simple, prosaic, but deeply important fact stands out. The process takes a great deal of time and effort. It is obvious, too, that while there are many committees and subcommittees, there is only one Secretary in each department; and the committees, quite naturally, want to discuss important matters with the Secretary.[4] On his part, the Secretary knows that he must do this, and do it effectively, if the policies of the administration are to be carried out. So the time spent in congressional meetings is spent—and, for the most part, well spent—in the performance of one of his most im-

[4] "[Senator] George confirmed that the group [Senate Foreign Relations Committee] had rejected Dulles' offer to send Department Counselor Douglas MacArthur II and Livingston T. Merchant, Assistant Secretary for European Affairs, to tell members what went on in last week's meeting.

" 'If the committee wants to hear Mr. Dulles and he wants to bring along his assistants when he testifies that will be all right,' George said." Washington *Post and Times Herald*, Feb. 6, 1956, p. 8.

portant duties. It is possible, I think, to arrive at a quantitative estimate of the time this duty requires.

On November 29, 1955, Secretary Dulles told us that he had met during his tenure of office "more than 100 times with bipartisan Congressional groups." [5] This seems to me quite normal practice.

As nearly as I can reconstruct it from my appointment books, I met during four years as Secretary on 214 occasions with these groups. One hundred twenty-five of these were formal committee meetings, usually stenographically reported. The remainder were informal meetings. Many committee meetings occupied half a day, measured from the Secretary's portal-to-portal (if more, each half-day is counted as a meeting). Informal meetings were usually shorter, running from an hour to two or three. In my experience preparation for meetings required at least as much time as the meetings themselves, usually more, since the ground which would be covered was never precisely predictable. I will not be far wrong, then, in estimating that each formal meeting took half a day and preparation half a day, or a total of 125 days; that each informal meeting took about one-quarter of a day. This is in the neighborhood of one-sixth of my working days in Washington. Periods of absence on international

[5] *Department of State Bulletin*, Dec. 12, 1955, pp. 965, 966.

conferences are excluded. There were, of course, additional and more relaxed opportunities for exchange of views on social occasions after working hours.

General figures cannot reflect the peaks of pressure which the work with Congress involves. There are occasions when not a sixth of the Secretary's time but all of it is occupied on the Hill. For instance, from June 1 to June 9, 1951, inclusive, I testified every day (except Sunday) and nearly all day before joint Senate committees investigating the relief of General MacArthur. Preparation began on May 8, with work, at the outset, chiefly at night, and continued every day until it filled pretty much the whole day. With these hearings concluded, I began preparation on June 22 for hearings before the House Committee on Foreign Affairs on the $8.5 billion foreign aid bill. The actual hearings occupied June 26, 27, and 28. So for this seven-week period, from May 11 to the end of June, fully half of the Secretary's time and energy was spent on work with congressional committees.

July and August, 1949, present an example of a diversity of matters crowded, indeed jumbled, together in a short time. July was the month of the publication of the China White Paper. It began with discussion with a number of individual Senators and

Congressmen interested in Chinese questions. These went on through the month. On the 20th and again on the 27th were lengthy meetings with the Joint Atomic Energy Committee in an attempt to clear the way for an improvement in our working relations in this field with Great Britain and Canada. Due to leaks and distorted publicity the effort failed.[6] The 28th was taken up with hearings on the military assistance program before the House Foreign Affairs Committee; and the 29th with prelim-

---

[6] This episode represents a typical hazard in dealing with Congress. In July, 1949, arrangements were made with Senator Brien McMahon (D., Conn.), Chairman of the Joint Atomic Energy Committee, for a meeting with the committee on July 20 to explore the matter. The proprieties of congressional protocol required that the ranking members of the committee and also of the committees dealing with foreign affairs and armed services be given prior and preferential information of what we wished to discuss. Invitations had been sent very privately to these men by President Truman, to meet in the evening of July 14 with him at Blair House. News of the meeting leaked. When the group gathered on a rainy night (the Secretaries of State and Defense, the Chairman of the Atomic Energy Commission, and General Eisenhower also attended), crowds of newspapermen and photographers were waiting on the sidewalk outside Blair House. Before the meeting ended, Senator Tydings of Maryland had to leave and was extensively interviewed on the steps. Various others contributed later in the evening. The newspaper reporting was extensive, speculative, and, in part, fanciful. The result was to annoy members not invited and so prejudice the discussions that, after an initial effort, they had to be abandoned.

inary discussion of the subject with the Chairmen of
the Senate Foreign Relations and Armed Services
Committees. On August 2 I appeared before a joint
meeting of these committees in the morning, returning to the House committee in the afternoon. After
a conference with Chairmen Connally and Kee on
August 4, the discussion with the joint Senate committees was resumed on the morning of the 5th, and
that with the House committee in the afternoon.
Public hearings before the joint Senate committees
took the morning of the 8th. I met President Quirino
of the Philippines, who arrived in the afternoon,
and talked with him on the 9th. The morning of the
10th was given over to an appearance before the
House Foreign Affairs Committee on the White
Paper, and the morning of the 11th to another meeting on military assistance. After two meetings on the
12th with Senator Vandenberg, I was able to turn
to other than congressional matters until the end of
the month, when the President and I met with
Senators George and Lucas to discuss problems
raised by the Reciprocal Trade Agreements Bill.

January, 1950, was another active month, with
fifteen meetings, nine committee appearances, and
eight informal meetings. The subjects covered included Formosa, complete surveys of our foreign
relations, the departmental budget for 1951, aid

to China, the Selective Service Bill, the All-American canal in the Southwest, Korea, and an appointment in which a member of Congress was interested.

In all these hours and days of meetings and consultations, as in all work, the moments of positive accomplishment, of forward movement, are disappointingly few. Much of the time is spent in what Secretary Stimson used to call "stopping rat holes." But that, too, is important work—as one finds out when it is neglected—even though it leaves the big tasks untouched. For instance, when Mr. Attlee came here in December, 1950, apprehension was expressed in the Senate that he and the President might enter into secret arrangements. Indeed, Senator Kem, for himself and twenty-three Republican Senators, introduced a resolution giving it as the sense of the Senate that the President at the close of the meetings should make a full and complete report on them to the Senate and that he should not enter into any understandings or agreements which might bind the United States.[7] This plainly was an infringement of the constitutional preroga-

[7] Senate Resolution 371, 81st Cong., 2d Sess., *Congressional Record*, Vol. 96, Part 12, p. 16173. Those joining in the resolution were Senators Wherry, Knowland, Bricker, Cain, Williams, Schoeppel, Aiken, Thye, Hendrickson, Mundt, Donnell, Brewster, Nixon, Butler, Malone, Dworshak, Young, Capehart, Watkins, Jenner, Cordon, McCarthy, and Ecton.

tive of the President to conduct negotiations with foreign nations.[8] In this case the issue was an unreal one, since it has become customary for the Secretary of State to meet with the foreign committee of each House after important international meetings and review developments with them. So on December 9 I attended a joint meeting of the two committees and discussed with them most amicably all that had taken place. Interest in the resolution was short-lived. On December 18, 1950, it was defeated by a vote of 45 to 30.[9]

These congressional meetings before and after an international conference, useful as they are, have a disadvantage which is part of the great glare of publicity thrown on all preparations for these conferences as well as upon the conferences themselves. Flexibility even in minor matters is much more difficult when, before a meeting, all possibilities are analyzed in public and positions publicly taken. Agreement requires that some, perhaps all, modify their attitudes to meet changes by others. A position publicly proclaimed is more rigid by reason

[8] "Into the field of negotiation [with foreign nations] the Senate cannot intrude; and Congress itself is powerless to invade it." *United States v. Curtiss-Wright Export Corp.*, 299 U.S. 304, 319 (1936).

[9] 81st Cong., 2d Sess., *Congressional Record*, Vol. 96, Part 12, p. 16691.

of its public nature. Furthermore, to announce all
one's positions in advance of the negotiation is apt
to make it merely a forum for reiterating final positions and not a true negotiation. But there are so
many contributors to this situation that it would be
unfair to attribute much of it to the liaison with
Congress.

The occasions when the executive and the Congress are brought together in the origination or the
development of policy are not found in these executive, and certainly not in the public, sessions of
congressional committees. The latter have an important and useful place in the democratic governmental process. But it is in the public examination
and criticism of proposed action. This both tests
what is proposed, and, through press, radio, and television coverage, informs the electorate in regard to
it. The creative process is both more individual and
more elusive because more private. And being individual, it cannot be stated in a formula. It is
secreted in the qualities of men. During his illness
I had the rare opportunity of many talks with Senator Vandenberg on this subject, wholly divorced
from any specific task. For many years I had observed him and worked with him. But these talks
were contemplative. We reviewed our experience
and tried to draw conclusions from it.

What then are the qualities in men and the posture of circumstances which make for this creative process, when policy is moved forward to a new phase? On the committee's side what is needed is a chairman or senior minority member who is widely respected and trusted in his own party. Such a man usually stands well with the opposition also. He must be able to think vigorously about new problems, though he need not have an original cast of mind. His great function is to bring suggestions within the realm of the possible, to use method as a means of molding a proposal to make it politically feasible. He will, of course, be a politician. He will protect the interests of his party, and perhaps of himself, so that what he becomes convinced is in the national interest is not done so as to injure his party or aggrandize its opponent. But he will not be tricky. What he requires as a condition of support will be frankly stated. He will keep in touch with his colleagues, particularly his own party colleagues, and have a pretty sound idea that what he agrees to back will have the needed support when the time for voting comes.

On the executive side what is needed is a man who can speak for the administration because he knows it and is trusted by it. He, too, must keep in touch, be frank and not tricky, and must pursue

the main objective without being deflected by the
nonessential. These two men must have confidence
in one another.

An example of this sort of collaboration occurred
in 1948 between Senator Vandenberg, then Chairman of the Foreign Relations Committee, and Mr.
Robert Lovett, Under Secretary of State, which
resulted in the Vandenberg Resolution, the pre-
cursor of the North Atlantic Treaty. Senator Vandenberg's position was unique. He was Chairman
of the committee; by understanding with Senator
Taft he was given the lead on the Republican side
in foreign affairs while Senator Taft had it in domestic affairs. His influence in both parties was
immense. He was a master of maneuver and a
superb advocate. He and Mr. Lovett trusted and
liked one another. Mr. Lovett could and did efface
himself from the public eye. His ability matched
the Senator's. He had at his finger tips the facts
and needs of the situation, the desired policy. Their
work together produced what neither could have
accomplished separately.

Examples of similar work on a much broader base
were the meetings which Mr. Hull held in 1944
with three separate groups from Congress in which
were discussed drafts of the United Nations Charter

prior to the Dumbarton Oaks Conference. Mr. Hull has described these fully.[10]

The Secretary met first on four occasions with eight members of the Senate Foreign Relations Committee. That committee was then organized with a view to having on it leaders of senatorial opinion. That it had is seen by the composition of the group—Senators Connally, Barkley, George, Gillette, Vandenberg, LaFollette, White, and Austin. But other Senators were interested in the Charter, too, and to draw them in without questioning the prerogative of the committee, the Secretary held a separate consultation with what was then known as the B2H2 group—Senators Ball, Burton, Hatch, and Hill. Since the House Committee on Foreign Affairs did not then normally include the party leaders in the House, the group invited to meet with the Secretary consisted of the Speaker and Majority Leader, Mr. Rayburn and Mr. McCormack, the Minority Leader, Mr. Martin, the Chairman and ranking minority member of the committee, Messrs. Bloom and Eaton, and Representatives Ramspeck and Arends. The Secretary also used his great influence, in the quiet way of which he was a master, to induce the national conventions of both parties to

[10] *The Memoirs of Cordell Hull* (The Macmillan Company, New York, 1948), Vol. II, p. 1657 *et seq.*

adopt planks favoring an international organization
to keep the peace.[11] This whole effort was outstand-
ingly successful—a classic example of persuasion
through participation by a man who thoroughly
understood congressional processes.

If these occasions of real accomplishment in cooperation are rare, they would be even more rare
were it not for the far larger number of meetings—
which are also the "oil of government," preventing
grievances from going unaired, preserving *amour
propre,* giving a sense of participation and an opportunity to exercise authority over detail.

It is often said that the executive must "get along"
with Congress and particularly with the Senate. If
this means that concessions of policy must be made
in the interest of outward affability, I do not agree.
Personal relations will for the most part be courteous
and friendly, as one would expect between gentlemen. But no one knows better than politicians and
lawyers that men can battle most bitterly in the
arena over important differences and yet maintain
amicable personal relations and cooperate on other
matters. The Eightieth Congress, with which President Truman had his fiercest battles, worked ad-
mirably in foreign affairs; and many of those who
demanded the dismissal of the Secretary of State in

[11] *Ibid.,* p. 1670.

1950-52 joined in passing all the major legislation he laid before the Congress, including the Japanese and German treaties on the very eve of the campaign of 1952. Mutual respect is more important than affability.

We return always, I think, to a central truth. The relations between the executive and legislative branches of our government were not designed to be restful. We must not be disturbed and think that things have gone amiss when power striking against power, and being restrained, produces sparks. Congress has, for instance, always wished to inquire into the internal processes by which a particular executive decision was reached; which employees had part in it; what advice each gave. The desire is natural, but to indulge it would destroy the administrative process and organization. If an employee is to do his unintimidated best, he must be shielded from the unequal struggle with a congressional investigation. The responsibility must be borne by those political officers upon whom it properly rests —the Secretary and his chief assistants, appointed by the President by and with the advice and consent of the Senate. I think the Congress understands the justice and necessity for a firm attitude here to preserve the integrity of the executive branch, and, though a refusal of such requests often produces momentary irritation, the issue is rarely pressed.

Secretary Stimson believed strongly in the desirability of a question period in the House and Senate on the British model, during which cabinet officers would appear on the floor and respond to questions submitted in advance. He was not alone in this. At the beginning of this government the practice was common. In July, 1789, the Secretary of Foreign Affairs, Mr. Jefferson, "attended, agreeably to order, and made the necessary explanations." [12] The Secretary of War, General Knox, appeared in August of the same year twice before the House, and, with President Washington, twice before the Senate.[13] The President was displeased with his reception and did not return. The Act of September 2, 1789,[14] creating the Treasury Department, provided (as the law still does)[15] that the Secretary was "to make report, and give information to either branch of the legislature, in person or in writing (as he may be required), respecting all matters referred to him by the Senate or House of Representatives, or which shall appertain to his office." The House discussed in 1790 whether Secretary Hamilton should make his report on the public credit in

[12] *Annals of Congress*, 1st Cong., Vol. 1, p. 51.
[13] *Ibid.*, pp. 684, 689, 66, 69.
[14] 1st Cong., 1st Sess., 1 Stat. 65, 66.
[15] U.S.C., Title 5, Sec. 242.

person or in writing and decided on the latter only because of the mass of detail involved.[16] Mr. Justice Story was a strong advocate of the right and duty of cabinet officers to appear on the floor both to answer questions and to participate in debate.[17] In 1864 a select committee of the House (vigorously supported by James A. Garfield) and in 1881 a select committee of the Senate (on which James G. Blaine served) recommended the right to the floor of both Houses for cabinet officers both to answer questions and to participate in debate.[18] In 1912 President Taft, in a message to Congress of December 19, made the same recommendation.[19]

The Pendleton Committee of 1881 concisely sums up the argument for its view:

This system will require the selection of the strongest men to be heads of departments, and will require them to be well equipped with the knowledge of their offices. It will also require the strongest men to be the leaders of Congress and participate in debate. It will bring these strong men in contact, perhaps into conflict, to

[16] *Annals of Congress*, 1st Cong., Vol. 1, pp. 1043-1044.

[17] Joseph Story, *Commentaries on the Constitution* (Bigelow Edition, Little, Brown and Company, Boston, 1905), Vol. I, Sec. 869 *et seq.*

[18] *U.S. House Reports*, 38th Cong., 1st Sess., Vol. 1, No. 43, April 6, 1864; *U.S. Senate Reports*, 46th Cong., 3d Sess., Vol. 1, No. 837, Feb. 4, 1881.

[19] 62d Cong., 3d Sess., *Congressional Record*, Vol. 49, Part I, pp. 895-896.

advance the public weal, and thus stimulate their abilities and their efforts, and will thus assuredly result to the good of the country.[20]

At one time I thought this proposal had more merit than I do now. It seems to me an ill-suited graft upon the committee system, on the one hand, and the presidential system, on the other. A Secretary who developed a capacity for congressional debate might well be in trouble on two sides. On one side he would be rivaling and diminishing the position of the chairman of the committee concerned. Out of this much trouble could grow. The other hazard, as Mr. Laski pointed out,[21] would be the development by cabinet officers of a status and interests independent of the President, reminiscent of Stanton's with President Johnson, another impediment in the way of unified administrative policy. I doubt, too, the assumption in the Pendleton report and in Mr. Justice Story's argument that the "strongest" men, "statesmen of high public character" best qualified for the administration of policy, are necessarily those best qualified for debate in Congress. Sometimes men are gifted in both en-

[20] *U.S. Senate Reports*, 46th Cong., 3d Sess., Vol. 1, No. 837, Feb. 4, 1881, p. 8.

[21] Harold J. Laski, *The American Presidency, an Interpretation* (Harper & Brothers, New York and London, 1940), p. 100 *et seq.*

deavors; but, as I have observed government for a good many years, it is as often, perhaps more often, not the case.

It is interesting that the Confederate Constitution had a provision permitting cabinet officers to sit in the Congress upon invitation. But the invitation was never issued, for fear that to do so might give the President too much power.[22]

More important, perhaps, than considerations which must remain theoretical is the fact that our chambers do not have the tradition of discipline in relevance which permits Mr. Speaker in the House of Commons to maintain strict control over the question period. In May, 1950, after a European conference, I had an experience of an informal congressional question period in an appearance before the members of both Houses in the auditorium of the Library of Congress. The questioning in this meeting seemed to bear out the misgivings I have expressed.[23]

[22] E. Merton Coulter, *The Confederate States of America, 1861-1865* (Louisiana State University Press, 1950), pp. 382-383.

[23] The meeting was arranged by President Truman to take place on my return from a NATO Council in London, at which the first steps were taken culminating later in the year in the unified NATO command under General Eisenhower. The President believed that the London developments were of interest to the whole Congress, not merely to members of the foreign com-

The architecture of our government is, I think, too set, practice has adapted it too well to our continental scope, to have it improved by additions or embellishments in the parliamentary style. The larger truth is that the two systems operate as *systems*—each with its general strength; each paying some price in weakness for the strength it has. To graft some special trait of the one onto the other, without regard either to the whole of the society it serves or to the whole legal and extra-legal framework into which it fits, will not produce better performance, but only a fracture, in the exercise of responsible power.

We have in this country been developing methods of our own by which, for instance, some members of the Congress can gain personal experience in foreign relations and in meeting and understanding the attitudes of foreign peoples and governments. The practice has grown up—and it is a good one— of having alternately two Senators and two Congressmen on the United States Delegation to the

mittees. I appeared, reported at some length, and was questioned. The questions related to a range of matters concerning our foreign relations, with scant attention to the London meeting.

In June, 1951, I was called to testify, as stated on page 66 above, regarding the relief of General MacArthur, before a joint meeting of two committees. The questioning went on for eight days and occupies 624 pages of the printed record. At the end of this inquisition the Chairman, Senator Russell of Georgia, said:

General Assembly of the United Nations. Subcommittees of the Senate and House Foreign Committees for geographical areas are kept closely in touch with developments in these areas. They often travel in these parts of the world when Congress is not in session. Indeed congressional travel is widespread and, for the most part, to the good. If sometimes a particular country seems to be subject to mass in-

---

"Mr. Secretary, I do not know whether it would be the source of either pride or consolation to you, but your examination here has been the most extensive of any witness who has been before a hearing that has become somewhat noted for the thoroughness not to mention the repetition of the examination.

"You have far exceeded in the number of questions, the number of words and the number of hours that you have been upon the stand the record of any previous witness. . . .

"We certainly have a better grasp of the many very staggering problems which confronted you during your tenure of office as Secretary of State and the steps that have been taken to meet them." Hearings before the Committee on Armed Services and the Committee on Foreign Relations United States Senate, 82d Cong., 1st Sess., to Conduct an Inquiry into the Military Situation in the Far East and the Facts Surrounding the Relief of General of the Army Douglas MacArthur from His Assignments in That Area, Part 3, pp. 2290-2291.

I have not again paged through this dreary record. To be required to do so would violate the constitutional guarantee against cruel and unusual punishment. But I venture the opinion that not more than an hour of the examination related to the relief of General MacArthur. The understanding of relevance continues to elude the gentlemen of Capitol Hill.

vasion, and if the inevitable press conference by the visitors rarely produces beneficial results, the price is not too heavy for the increase in understanding which comes with personal experience.

Today it is of new and pressing importance that the House have understanding of foreign affairs. The time has passed when the Senate monopolized the congressional function in this field, since it is the execution of policy, calling for legal authority, funds, and men, which is the ultimate test of success or failure. The importance of the House in this field has grown and is growing, presenting new problems of giving information and a sense of participation to so large a membership. I venture to say that, if it were possible to assess the factors which led to the erroneous Soviet judgment of our probable reaction to the invasion of South Korea, the defeat in the House of the Korean Aid Bill (H.R. 5330) on January 19, 1950, would bulk large.[24] The North Korean radio

[24] The bill was defeated by a vote of 192 (132 Republicans, 59 Democrats, 1 American Labor) to 191 (170 Democrats and 21 Republicans). Among those voting against the bill were Richard Nixon (Cal.), Case (S. Dak.), Chiperfield (Ill.), Halleck (Ind.), Vorys (Ohio), Wolcott (Mich.), Marcantonio (N.Y.). Those in favor of it included Mrs. Bolton (Ohio), Fulton (Pa.), Furcolo (Mass.), Herter (Mass.), Jackson (Wash.), Javits (N.Y.), Kennedy (Mass.), Mansfield (Mont.), Merrow (N.H.), Monroney (Okla.), Ribicoff (Conn.), Roosevelt (N.Y.). 81st Cong., 2d Sess., *Congressional Record*, Vol. 96, Part 1, p. 656.

gave the action prominent attention, quoting a member of the House to the effect that aid to Korea was "pouring money down a rat hole." Would it seem likely in Moscow that a nation would come to the military assistance of another which its popular assembly had been unwilling to aid with funds?

In the years in which I was associated with it the House Committee on Foreign Affairs was a hard-working and understanding committee. Its security and its staff were excellent. The committee did not carry the same weight in the House as did its counterpart in the Senate, so that unanimity became of special importance. A vociferous minority could make any result unpredictable. One of the masters of producing a unanimous committee without injury to the policy put forward was the late Congressman Bloom of New York, its Chairman for many years.

All that I have said about legislative-executive relations in the field of my experience can be summed up in a few sentences. It is not easy to conduct our foreign relations in the national interest with the limitations imposed by democratic political practices. A good deal of wear and tear will occur on the executive side, and it had best be liberally supplied with spare parts. Of all my principal assistants at the beginning of four years only one remained at the end. I found a rest not unwelcome myself.

On the legislative side, a great danger, as in military operations, is to underestimate the problem. Legislators would do well to repeat to themselves: it is not as simple as we think. But the job can be done; and, if one would look for the "oil of government" which is of most help in the common task, it might be found in two quiet qualities, not much touted in politics, humility and disinterestedness.

IV

PROGNOSIS

Among the manifold uncertainties of this life, I
venture one prediction. If, at the present time, the
limitation imposed by democratic political practices makes it difficult to conduct our foreign affairs
in the national interest, this difficulty will increase,
and not decrease, with the years. The problem is
not merely the one which de Tocqueville pointed
out, though that persists. "As for myself," he wrote,
"I do not hesitate to say that it is especially in the
conduct of their foreign relations that democracies
appear to me decidedly inferior to other governments. . . . Foreign politics demand scarcely any
of those qualities which are peculiar to a democracy; they require, on the contrary, the perfect use
of almost all those in which it is deficient. . . . [A]
democracy can only with great difficulty regulate
the details of an important undertaking, persevere

in a fixed design, and work out its execution in spite
of serious obstacles. It cannot combine its measures
with secrecy or await their consequences with patience. These are qualities which more especially
belong to an individual or an aristocracy." [1]

To this something else is added. In the first place,
the questions to be understood, and then solved,
have vastly increased in complexity and dimension.
They have taken on technical aspects requiring
knowledge rare even among the intellectually elite.
They involve the collection and analysis of information so current that it is changing in the very process
of collection. How different was the leisurely pace
when Secretary of State Thomas Jefferson wrote
to William Carmichael, the American Chargé
d'Affaires at Madrid, in March, 1791: "Your letter
of May 6. 1789. is still the last we have received, &
that is now near two years old. . . . A full explanation of the causes of this suspension of all information from you, is expected in answer to my letter of
Aug. 6 [1790]. It will be waited for yet a reasonable
time, & in the mean while a final opinion sus-
pended." [2]

---

[1] De Tocqueville, *Democracy in America*, Vol. I, pp. 234-235.
[2] *The Works of Thomas Jefferson* (Federal Edition, G. P. Put-
nam's Sons, The Knickerbocker Press, New York, 1904), Vol. VI,
pp. 221-222.

In the second place, the task of understanding and solving these questions requires the coordinated work of many minds with diverse training and competence, so that innumerable facts and considerations may be held in solution until the moment for the catalyst of decision. This sort of attack the Congress by its organization and history is incapable of making. Sir Harold Nicolson has described Mr. Dwight Morrow's mind as a pack of beagles, running back and forth in apparently hopeless confusion in search of the scent, and then, when one has found it, streaming off together in full cry. But the Congress is not a pack. Each committee picks up a scent of its own seeking, and off they all go in every conceivable direction. Among its many qualities Congress does not have the power of concentration, nor does, nor can, it have command of competence necessary to distill the significance from a mass of raw and confusing material.

The problems of today and tomorrow are different in their very nature from those of the heyday of democratic theory, the eighteenth century, just as the content of man's knowledge is different. It is, perhaps, not too great an illusion to believe that even at the end of the eighteenth century a man of capacity and zest could keep pretty well abreast of what was being done in the arts and sciences. The

trend which began in the middle of the seventeenth
century did not culminate for over a century and a
half. Of Western Europe in the period 1630-1650,
a scholar writes: "Gradually, the marvellous complexity of Elizabethan life was vanishing, the strands
of learning were being separated so that each
could be closely examined, compared to the next,
and put to use. The shift of interest was from meta-
physics to physics, from Being to Becoming. In
short, the age of specialization was just beginning." [3]
A Franklin or a Jefferson was not a stranger in any
field of learning. A gifted amateur could still hold
his own with the professionals. And the legislative
assembly was, above anything else, an assembly of
amateurs. Politics was not yet a profession. If politicians had any profession it was likely to be law;
and lawyers were the greatest jacks of all trades, the
greatest amateurs, of them all. The subjects governments dealt with did not seem alien or formidable
in complexity to these amateurs. [4] Military policy

[3] R. T. Petersson, *Sir Kenelm Digby* (Harvard University
Press, Cambridge, 1956), p. 119.

[4] Of 95 members of the First Congress who served full or part
terms, 53 were associated with the law, as practitioners, judges,
or students. The other members are listed, some as doctors,
ministers, planters, bankers, as engaging in mercantile pursuits,
and a number as having no designated profession; one sea
captain; one "a master of many trades" and teacher. The biog-
raphy of one Hugh Williamson of North Carolina shows, to be

(the militia, an army and a navy), education (a
system of common schools, higher education would
take care of itself), encouragement of inventions (a
system of patents), finance (Hamilton's theory was
simplicity itself compared with Keynes's), and so
on, were matters with which some or all of the

---

sure, that a non-lawyer could also master a wide range of knowledge, activity, and travel. "Born on Oterara Creek, in West Not-
tingham Township, Pa., December 5, 1735; attended the common schools; prepared for college at Newark, Del., and was
graduated from the University of Pennsylvania at Philadelphia
in 1757; studied theology, and was licensed to preach in 1758;
resigned, owing to ill health, in 1760; professor of mathematics
in the College of Philadelphia; studied medicine in Edinburgh,
Scotland, and Utrecht, Holland; returned to Philadelphia and
practiced there until 1773; became a member of the American
Philosophical Society, and was sent abroad as a member of the
commission to observe the transits of Venus and Mercury in
1773; at the time of 'The Boston Tea Party' he was examined
in England by the privy council regarding it; returned to America in 1776 and settled in Edenton, N.C.; engaged in mercantile
pursuits; during the Revolutionary War was surgeon general of
the North Carolina troops 1779-1782; member of the State
house of commons in 1782; Member of the Continental Congress
1782-1785, 1787, and 1788; delegate to the convention which
framed the Federal Constitution in 1787 and a member of the
State convention which adopted it in 1789; elected as a Federal-
ist to the First and Second Congresses . . . moved to New York
City in 1793; engaged extensively in literary pursuits until his
death in New York City, May 22, 1819; interment in the Apthorp
tomb in Trinity Churchyard." *Biographical Directory of the
American Congress, 1774-1949* (U.S. Gov't Printing Office,
1950), pp. 49-51, 2023.

assembly had more or less experience. To none were they shadowy and portentous mysteries where almost anything might be true, lands about which the most bizarre tales of a returning Marco Polo were entirely credible.

Even when the majority of Americans were farmers, the "science of agriculture" and the government's part in furthering it were meager. Until 1862, agriculture had no representative in any of the departments of government except for one clerk in the Patent Office—whose job was to register the invention of farm implements. A Department of Agriculture was created by Congress on May 15, 1862, but its chief officer was a commissioner of agriculture, who was not brought into the cabinet until 1889. The vast and complex scientific work of the Department of Agriculture really dates from the Wilson Administration.

Nowhere is the age of the amateur more clearly reflected than in the military establishment where the main reliance of the nation's defense was placed on the militia. The standing army was so small that at the turn of the twentieth century annual maneuvers had to be cancelled since there weren't enough troops to maneuver. Moreover, it was not until the first years of the twentieth century that a General Staff was established.

But today how small is the comfortable and familiar area of our intellectual globe, how vast the unknown! As the amateur, whether in or out of Congress, begins to think of the nature and extent of dangers to our national life and ways to meet them, he runs into difficulty at the very start. The crudest danger, the easiest to understand as an idea, is that from foreign force. But is it easy to understand as a fact? If we cannot fully understand, at least we can dimly grasp the immensity of the destruction wrought by thermo-nuclear bombs. But the facts regarding capability of delivering these bombs on target and defense against this—both the active defense of intercepting and destroying the attacker and the passive defense of minimizing the effect of the blow—are more complicated and more problematical. Here enter such technical matters as early warning and interceptor systems, guided missiles launched from the ground and from the air and from surface craft and submarines, and, in the background, still to be developed, intercontinental ballistic missiles. By and large, the amateur, skeptical of extravagant claims, can gather that the development of the defense is well behind that of the offense, and not gaining appreciably; that whether the objective of the attack is the enemy's air force or his centers of population and industry, the latter are likely to suffer heavily and the former is not apt to be rendered incapable of retaliating strongly enough to cause destruction about equal to that of the attack, barring accidents. But this is small comfort to the Congressman whose basic role is control of the purse strings. How much money shall he grant to whom and for what? How much for offense? How much for defense? And who are the proper guardians of offense, the Air Force alone, or the Air Force and the Navy together? [5]

Nor is this all, for the suspicion begins to dawn that if nuclear weapons and delivery power are a

[5] In October, 1949, the revolt of the Admirals, set off by Capt. John G. Crommelin Jr.'s unauthorized release to newspapers of confidential letters, and including among its participants Admirals Denfeld, Radford, Ofstie, Blandy, Halsey, Nimitz, Bogan, and Kinkaid, exposed basic differences of strongly held convictions among the services, particularly the Navy and Air Force. Congressional hearings were held, in which the Navy, smarting under the cancellation of its proposed giant air-carrier the *United States*, and the bearing of this upon the future defensive and offensive power of the United States, questioned the basic military decisions involved in the choice of the B-36 plane (after a previous congressional investigation of motives of those ordering its production and purchase) as the vehicle of United States strategic air bombing. The state of Navy morale, the capabilities of the B-36 as compared with carrier-based planes, the effectiveness and the morality of atomic bombing, and the right of any one service to pronounce on the weapons of another were among the matters challenged. The Agenda of the House Armed Services Committee for the hearings included the following:

deterrent against resort to force, they are not a
deterrent operative in all circumstances. They are
calculated to deter only those uses of force which
are likely, in the shrewd judgment of an adversary
who is not stupid, to steel us to loose nuclear attack
with the certainty of nuclear reprisal. To do this we
must believe that a national interest of the most
vital importance is imperiled. If it is true, as is
not unlikely, that were the present, or soon attainable, stockpiles (Soviet, British, and American) all
exploded, they would gravely imperil all life on this

"1. Examine the performance characteristics of the B-36
bomber to determine whether it is a satisfactory weapon.

"2. Examine the roles and missions of the Air Force and
the Navy (especially Navy Aviation and Marine Aviation) to
determine whether or not the decision to cancel the con-
struction of the aircraft carrier United States was sound.

"3. Establish whether or not the Air Force is concentrating
upon strategic bombing to such an extent as to be injurious
to tactical aviation and the development of adequate fighter
aircraft and fighter aircraft techniques.

"4. * * *

"5. Study the effectiveness of strategic bombing to determine whether the nation is sound in following the concept
to the present extent.

"6. * * *" New York Times, Oct. 6, 1949, p. 17.

During the hearings the Navy cited experience in World War
II to show the inappropriateness of relying on strategic bombing
from land bases to the extent called for by the decisions of the
Department of Defense. General Vandenberg, on the other side,

planet, then the deterrent value of these weapons is to deter their own use. In any event it becomes clear that to rely solely on nuclear power to deter or meet the use of force is to require a do-all or do-nothing alternative which must result, except in dire extremity, in doing nothing. Therefore, military capability, other than nuclear, becomes a necessity.

But again the questions arise: How much, of what sort, and with what division of funds between nuclear offense and defense and more "conven-

---

maintained that the Navy had "recommended that we cancel out this country's capability of conducting a strategic offensive with atomic weapons," and that this would "destroy the one greatest equalizing factor in the balance of military power between a potential enemy and the western democracies." *New York Times*, Oct. 20, 1949, p. 4. At least one of the participants in the argument later found himself on the opposite side. "The witness [Radford] denounced the B-36 primarily as the 'symbol' and vehicle of what he declared was an Air Force theory of war that falsely led the public to assume that it promised 'a cheap and easy victory if war should come.' . . . The committee and country must determine whether to permit this 'morally reprehensible' concept, he declared." *New York Times*, Oct. 8, 1949, p. 2. All of this indicates that these questions are not easy to decide, nor do they stay decided in the rapid rush of time.

The *New York Times* summed the matter up on October 23 (Section 4, p. E-1): "The basic questions at issue in the 'Battle of the Pentagon' are these: What kind of defense 'unification' should the nation have? Should the views of one branch of the armed services be subject to veto by the others? If a war comes how should America fight it?"

tional" forces? Here it is difficult in the extreme for the layman to get the facts on which to base an informed opinion—or to understand those which he does get. Some of the necessary information is unobtainable either because security—our own and other nations'—cannot be penetrated, or because no one knows the facts. Some information is so bent and twisted by special interest and controversy that the layman cannot get it straight. Only a substantial and highly competent staff under strong leadership concerned solely with getting at the truth, uninhibited by barriers of secrecy and with power to compel the production of data, can work its way through the obstructions of the sincere—and not so sincere—interests and disagreements of the three armed services, the atomic energy authorities, those who insist on the reduction of expenditures, and those who wish to claim this or that achievement in foreign or domestic affairs. One may suspect that even the President may have the greatest difficulty in getting a true report of such information as is obtainable, because so many of his subordinates have so great a vested interest in obscuring it.[6] Cer-

[6] The difficulty is vastly increased when a President expects his subordinates to present him with "agreed recommendations." A good many years of experience have convinced me that this is a thoroughly pernicious practice. Agreement is reached at the lowest common denominator of those agreeing. The method is

tainly he cannot get it without the aid of some such group as I have mentioned.

If this is so, the task of a congressional committee to obtain a solid foundation for judgment on the adequacy of military programs presented by the executive branch is a formidable one indeed. Essential prerequisites are thorough organization and preparation for the work, faithful attendance by committee members at time-consuming hearings, and

---

not to resolve differences, but to obscure them by generalization. The greater the basic disagreement, the more general and vague the "agreed recommendation" which each believes will permit the course upon which he is determined. The result is that the President is not aware that an issue exists calling for his authoritative decision, and is not informed of the considerations which he should weigh in deciding it. The desire to "spare the President" differences of opinion may well deprive him of his chief duty and role. He is the decider-in-chief. There is a large element of the judicial in his role. The greatest service his subordinates can render him is to sharpen issues and inform him of the pros and cons, not cover them up and leave him in the dark. A President's counselors should ponder Francis Bacon's words: "The greatest trust between man and man is the trust of giving counsel. For in other confidences men commit the parts of life; their lands, their goods, their child, their credit, some particular affair; but to such as they make their counsellors, they commit the whole: by how much the more they are obliged to all faith and integrity. . . . The counsels at this day in most places are but familiar meetings, where matters are rather talked on than debated. And they run too swift to the order or act of counsel." *Works of Francis Bacon,* "Essay XX, Of Counsel" (Longman & Co., London, 1858), Vol. VI, pp. 423, 426.

the complete avoidance by staff and members of sensationalism. An excellent example of effective investigation has been given by the Subcommittee on the Air Force (Symington Committee) of the Committee on Armed Services of the Senate, appointed during the Eighty-fourth Congress by Senator Russell to inquire into the capacity of the Air Force under "present policies, legislative authority, and appropriations" to carry out its "assigned missions." The committee, whose hearings have been published, carried out its investigation in an exemplary way. As I write, its report has not been made, but it should furnish a real test of congressional competence in this particularly exacting field. One would like to believe, but I fear cannot, that the Congress was more convinced by the hearings of this subcommittee than it was impelled by annoyance with Secretary of Defense Wilson when it gave the Air Force funds, which it took away from the foreign aid program, and thus got a double satisfaction and release from frustration.

For, though the inquiry into national security begins with the military equations, it does not end there. Power is by no means wholly a matter of force. If the Soviet Union and the United States engage in hurling atomic destruction at one another across intercontinental space, then other nations can play no role except that of victims of *Götter-dämmerung*. But it is a postulate of policy to avoid this extremity, to shape conduct to prevent general suicide. In any policy which will protect both our existence and our civilization (the sort of existence which has value for us), other nations are of the greatest importance. So long as there is mutual abstention from the use of nuclear weapons, the present power of the Western nations and the Sino-Soviet bloc is sufficiently equal to produce a sort of kinetic equilibrium in which major physical aggressive moves are unlikely. This power flows from a combination of population, resources, technology, and plant which will produce results in a number of material fields (economic and military) calculated to inspire respect and attraction.

In this situation two conclusions must be self-evident. One is that major defections from one group to the other will produce shifts of power which could have decisive consequences. Hence a major object of policy of each group or coalition, if it is conscious of its interests, must be to strengthen and cement its own group and weaken and divide the opposing group. The second conclusion is that the power of the uncommitted peoples (in Asia, South, and Southeast Asia, the Middle East, and Africa), very considerable and growing as an absolute matter, is of critical importance if thrown into the scales. Thus to each group the neutrality of the uncommitted peoples is a minimum requirement, and their friendly support, with a sense of common interest, is a highly desired end. It is the Soviet recognition of this truth and the increasing reorientation of its policy toward it since the Nineteenth Communist Party Congress in October, 1952, which has so disorganized and confused Western policy.

So the legislator passes from the problems posed by the use or threat of physical force, tangled and technical in the extreme, to the even more abstruse questions raised by that whole area of power which does not rest on force—but which may condition it. Here are involved factors of the growth of productive power, of the degree of conviction of a society in its philosophic and spiritual foundations, of the relations between peoples of radically different racial, historical, and cultural backgrounds and at many levels of economic condition and stages of development. To the amateur the problems of nuclear war seem much more complicated and difficult than those of competitive coexistence. He is probably wrong about this, not because the complexities of the former are less than he thinks, but because the complexities of the latter are far greater and our knowledge of them less.

For here we leave whatever exactitude may reside in the physical sciences and launch into the imponderables of man's behavior. Suppose, for instance—as seems to be true—that the productive power of the Soviet Union is growing far faster than the more mature economic systems of the West, and perhaps faster than any society of which we have records, what do we conclude from this? We know many of the reasons—the jump from a peasant society into the latest industrial techniques developed by others, the forced austerity in consumption to permit production of capital goods, and so on. But will the rate of development, or anything like it, continue? When will the U.S.S.R.'s production exceed that of the U.S.A.? What will be the curve of China's industrialization? What will be the effect of such a shift in the ratio of productive power on military capabilities? On capability for economic and political maneuvering? On the attraction of the Communist bloc for the uncommitted peoples? Is it desirable to attempt to accelerate our own growth in productive power? How? For what immediate purposes? These questions, I submit, are quite as important and quite as difficult as those in the realm of nuclear physics. They are equally out of the field of competence of the amateur.

But to him they do not seem to be. Although the

furthest marches of this territory may be trackless wilderness to him, it begins pretty close to the back pasture of the home farm. For twenty years as a trustee of a university I have noticed that the governing body, for the most part businessmen, lawyers, and clergymen—amateurs in education—wisely and passively accept the recommendations of the university administration, on faculty appointments and so on, in the scientific departments. But one can sense the restless consciousness of competence to criticize when attention turns to the departments of economics, history, law, or religion. We may not know even the criteria for determining who is sound and who is flighty in biochemistry, but we have our own ideas on deficit financing—or think we have until the government shows signs of stopping it. Here we, and the legislator, whose position—frustrations and all—is very like that of a member of a board of trustees, incur grave risks. Our ignorance is far greater than our consciousness of it.

The response of the amateur to these infinitely puzzling complexities is a typically human one. Man, so the anthropologists tell us, does not, like other mammals, adapt himself to his environment. He adapts his environment to himself. In cold climates, for instance, he does not grow his own coat; he takes some other creature's coat, covers himself with it,

and creates his own thermos container. A little ˙
later he utilizes a cave and fire to expand around him
a dry and warm environment. He does the same with
the situations we have been discussing. If they are
too complicated for his knowledge and experience,
he simplifies them until they begin to resemble the
facts of his personal and familiar world and then
applies in his thinking the experience and values of
that world.

"The practice of Americans," wrote de Tocqueville, "leads their minds to other habits, to fixing the
standard of their judgment in themselves alone. As
they perceive that they succeed in resolving without assistance all the little difficulties which their
practical life presents, they readily conclude that
everything in the world may be explained, and that
nothing in it transcends the limits of the understanding. Thus they fall to denying what they cannot comprehend; which leaves them but little faith
for whatever is extraordinary and an almost insur-
mountable distaste for whatever is supernatural." [7]

A foreign nation, for instance, is made up of a
considerable number of people, all to some extent
—sometimes to a great extent—different from us
and from one another. These people live in a different part of the world with different characteristics

[7] De Tocqueville, *Democracy in America,* Vol. II, p. 4.

from our part of it. Their experience has been different from ours; their conceptions are different; they have different fears and different aspirations from ours. Generally they have a common bond which makes them feel in some ways closer to people very different from themselves in their own country than to people more like themselves in other countries.

It is by no means simple to think realistically about these distant and alien communities, to act wisely in our relations with them. More knowledge is needed than the amateur can be expected to have. As a result he simplifies the problems; adapts the international environment to conceptions which cannot be adapted to it. Nations are personified and given the characteristics and qualities of individuals, out of experience with whom his own conceptions have been formed. Nations become brave, bullying, or cowardly; grasping or generous; moody, morose, stolid, gay, or irresponsible; logical or emotional; hard working or lazy; grateful for help or cynically contemptuous of an "easy touch," and so on. Their conduct is judged in the light of our individual experience with the conduct of individuals; and response is conceived of in the same vein. If Americans are seized and imprisoned, arbitrarily or on suspicion, by a Communist country, members of the press and the Congress demand that the State Department "do something and not just talk." Unfortunately "just talk" is about the only form of doing something which falls within the bounds of practicability; and, over a period, it is apt to be effective. But what is wanted is a "show-down." Those making this demand are neither clear nor in agreement as to what sort of a showdown they have in mind, but it is a mixture of an appeal to the force of a higher authority—"I'll sue you and take the case to the Supreme Court, if necessary"—and of the action taken when a neighborhood boy bullied your small brother.

So deep-seated is this personification of foreign populations that, in making foreign policy, legislators think of them, not as they think of large groups of people in their own country, but as they think of individuals among their own acquaintance. No member of Congress would urge a farm program which required, as a condition of benefits, agreements to support the party in power or not to support the opposing party, or which provided that benefits would be cut off from farmers who did support the opposing party. Legislators know that the farm group will continue to exist, whether they like it or not, that it is to their interest to influence it, and that threats only influence if and as long as the object of the threat must yield to it. So legislators do not threaten farmers or upbraid them for ingratitude. Rebuffs only challenge their ingenuity in persuasion.

But when the legislator thinks about foreigners, a wholly different set of conceptions takes command. To be sure foreigners don't vote and this is, perhaps, the dominant cause of the changed attitude; but it does not make the change in attitude toward a group of people as a group any more sensible. Foreign groups do not respond to threats any differently than domestic groups, and they, too, will continue to exist and be important to us. But the approach to the problem is wholly different.

That the power of the uncommitted peoples, if thrown into the scales, might be decisive, and that the only sort of world system which will command their support and loyalty is one in which they may within measurable time improve their lot—these ideas simply do not carry conviction. They would be the ABC's of politics if the legislator were thinking of the labor vote, or the farm vote. But with foreign nations assistance is not even equated with the Community Chest. The conception is that of a gift from one individual to another. And the normal and proper response expected from the recipient is gratitude to and support for the interests of the

giver. If at the next opportunity to return the favor
the beneficiary does not respond, still worse if he
takes a critical or hostile attitude, indignation is
great. He is said to have bitten the hand that feeds
him. But gratitude is not all that is expected. Proper
conduct for a recipient of gifts is to be frugal and
hard working, to have his budget (including the
gifts) balanced, and not to waste his substance on
loose living and frivolous diversions, among which
the welfare state is one.

To leave as little as possible to chance Congress
provides agreements for the prospective recipient to
sign; [8] enacts legislation to stop all gifts, and indeed,

[8] For instance:
"§ 1852. Agreements by recipient nations
"(a) No assistance shall be furnished to any nation under
this subchapter unless such nation shall have agreed to—

"(1) join in promoting international understanding and
good will, and maintaining world peace;
"(2) take such action as may be mutually agreed upon to
eliminate causes of international tension;
"(3) fulfill the military obligations, if any, which it has
assumed under multilateral or bilateral agreements or treaties
to which the United States is a party;
"(4) make, consistent with its political and economic stabil-
ity, the full contribution permitted by its manpower, resources,
facilities, and general economic condition to the development
and maintenance of its own defensive strength and the defensive strength of the free world;
"(5) take all reasonable measures which may be needed
to develop its defense capacities;

loans, to recipients who carry on trade of which it disapproves.[9] These attempts to compel what cannot be compelled do much to blight the purposes of the aid. Instead of persuading the uncommitted nations that the free world system holds the best promise for their independent development, they appear as attempts to re-entangle these countries in policies and purposes which are not theirs.

"(6) take appropriate steps to insure the effective utilization of the assistance furnished under this subchapter in furtherance of the policies and purposes of this subchapter;

"(7) impose appropriate restrictions against transfer of title to or possession of any equipment and materials, information, or services furnished under sections 1811-1818 of this title, without the consent of the President;

"(8) maintain the security of any article, service, or information furnished under sections 1811-1818 of this title;

"(9) furnish equipment and materials, services, or other assistance consistent with the Charter of the United Nations, to the United States or to and among other nations to further the policies and purpose of sections 1811-1818 of this title;

"(10) permit continuous observation and review by United States representatives of programs of assistance authorized under this title, including the utilization of any such assistance and provide the United States with full and complete information with respect to these matters, as the President may require." Mutual Security Act of 1954, 83d Cong., 2d Sess., 68 Stat. 832, 839, *as amended*, 84th Cong., 2d Sess., 69 Stat. 283, 285.

[9] See Mutual Defense Assistance Control Act of 1951, 82d Cong., 1st Sess., 65 Stat. 644 *et seq*.

An interesting clinic in this form of congressional direction of

Another form taken by the urge to simplify a situation too complex for ready understanding is the scapegoat simplification. This, too, involves high costs in harmful conduct at home and abroad. But it proceeds from one of the most deep-seated beliefs of primitive peoples—the belief in witchcraft. If things go persistently wrong with no simple and satisfying explanation, the mind finds explana-

---

foreign affairs is furnished by the following legislation regulating aid to Yugoslavia, a nation whose conduct and influence produces the gravest problems for the high command in the Kremlin:

"§143. Notwithstanding any other provision of law, no assistance under this title or any other title of this Act, or under any provision of law repealed by section 542(a) of this Act, shall be furnished to Yugoslavia after the expiration of ninety days following the date of the enactment of this section, unless the President finds and so reports to the Congress, with his reasons therefor, (1) that there has been no change in the Yugoslavian policies on the basis of which assistance under this Act has been furnished to Yugoslavia in the past, and that Yugoslavia is independent of control by the Soviet Union, (2) that Yugoslavia is not participating in any policy or program for the Communist conquest of the world, and (3) that it is in the interest of the national security of the United States to continue the furnishing of assistance to Yugoslavia under this Act." Public Law 726, c. 627, 84th Cong., 2d Sess., July 18, 1956.

On October 15, 1956, President Eisenhower made his required public pronouncement on this ticklish question. He found that Yugoslav independence was still threatened by the Soviet Union but more subtly than before and that the Yugoslavs were still defending it. They were reliable enough to get economic

tion in the occult, in spells evoked by those upon
whom disfavor has fallen for other reasons—in
short, by witches and witchcraft. The way to stop
the mischief is to root out the witches.

The resort to this simplification in popular thinking about foreign affairs is aided by another factor—

---

aid, but not jets and heavy equipment, and the whole situation
would be kept under constant review and control. See *New
York Times,* Oct. 16, 1956, p. 4.

Two days later the Yugoslav government came back with
what the *New York Times* understandably calls a "tart reaction."
It contained the following paragraphs:

"2. It results from the statement of President Eisenhower,
first of all, that the extension of partial economic aid is of
indefinite duration and can be revised at any moment.

"This presents great insecurity since it is always possible, for
one or another reason, to delay or cancel its further extension.

"It is the duty of every Government to provide its in-
habitants with regular supplies and it must know when and
with what it can count on what is of basic importance for
its planning.

"It is not possible to guarantee this in the way stated in the
report of the President.

"3. It is stated in the report that aid is being given to
enable Yugoslavia to preserve her independence.

"We consider that there exists no threat to the independence
of Yugoslavia on the part of the Soviet Union.

"We adhere consistently to the principles of our policy of
cooperation with all countries on an equal basis.

"Unfortunately, the report contains elements that are not
in conformity with the principles of independent and equal
cooperation." *New York Times,* Oct. 18, 1956, p. 3.

This is certainly carrying on foreign relations the hard way.

general misconceptions about the nature and extent of our national power. Twice we have seen this country turn its science, industry, and manpower to the business of war and smash the most formidable military machines which the world had yet seen. Our power amazed even ourselves. It was an easy step from the realization that it was very great to the belief that it was omnipotent.[10] But the step was as wrong as it was easy. And it was wrong chiefly because it assumed that force was the same thing as power, and that the nation which could lick all—well, almost all—others could acomplish anything it wished in its relations with them.[11] Many who did not think of power as deriving from force found its source in morality, and, "Thinking of power in moral terms, they overestimated their own influence and underestimated that of others." [12] "As the cold war dragged on, with the Communist success in China and the apparently permanent Sovietization of Eastern Europe, increasing numbers among

[10] See Denis Brogan, "The Illusion of American Omnipotence," *Harper's Magazine,* December, 1952.

[11] For a discussion of the difference in the nature of force and power and of their uses in the conduct of a nation's foreign affairs, see Louis J. Halle, *Civilization and Foreign Policy* (Harper & Brothers, New York, 1955), particularly Chapters VI, VII, VIII.

[12] Norman A. Graebner, *The New Isolationism* (The Ronald Press Co., New York, 1956), p. vi.

politicians and the general public began to lose patience. On the old assumption of limitless power, they could find only one explanation for the seeming failures of foreign policy—incompetence and even betrayal by successive administrations. The resulting outbreak of charges and investigations was firmly based on the old concepts of invincibility, moralism, and utopianism." [13]

That, in recent years, ambitious and unscrupulous men have played on this popular weakness and fanned it into a hysteria not equaled since the early days of the Massachusetts Bay Colony only attests its importance. "If," writes Professor Graebner, "the United States had found the task of subduing the revolution in Asia beyond its capabilities, it did not mean that Asia had unleashed a new energy. It meant simply that the State Department was full of Communists. McCarthy had invented the scapegoat of collective treason and employed it, as Hans J. Morgenthau has written, 'to reconcile the delusion of our omnipotence with the experience of limited power.'

"Taft and much of the Republican Party moved into line behind the Wisconsin Senator. . . .

"Soon Taft was speaking of the 'continuous sympathy toward communism . . . which inspired Amer-

[13] *Ibid.*, p. vi.

ican policy.' Whether Taft actually believed this or
not, he encouraged McCarthy to 'keep talking, and
if one case doesn't work out,' he added, 'proceed
with another.' The Republican Party shifted rapidly
toward the endorsement of these attacks, and in the
Republican Policy Committee statement of March,
1950, Taft admitted that the 'reaction seems to be
pretty good on the whole.' " [14]

This doctrine that our unlimited power has been
frustrated and rendered impotent before the puny
efforts of contemptible adversaries was made the
official Republican party line when Mr. Dulles supplied the laying on of hands in the platform of 1952.
There he set forth again the whole mythology—the
"tragic blunders" of Teheran, Yalta, and Potsdam,
the substitution "on our Pacific flank [of] a mur-
derous enemy for an ally and friend"; "the negative,
futile and immoral policy of 'containment' which
abandons countless human beings to a despotism
and Godless terrorism, which in turn enables the
rulers to forge the captives into a weapon for our
destruction." And what was the cause of all this
trouble? There was nothing complicated about the
answer; it was the "corruption, incompetence, and
disloyalty in public office" exhibited by the administration; it was the "hordes of loafers, incompetents

[14] *Ibid.*, pp. 29-30.

and unnecessary employes who clutter the administration of our foreign affairs." The platform proposed to sweep all this away, and with "dynamic initiative" achieve its program of unlimited objectives abroad, and at the same time a "balanced budget, a reduced national debt, an economical administration and a cut in taxes."

How all this passed beyond the empty bombast of what Wendell Willkie described as "only campaign oratory" when General Eisenhower, who the Scripps-Howard press had said was "running like a dry creek," succumbed to the lure of the McCarthy-Taft appeal and thereby to the right-wingers whom he had defeated for the nomination, and how the commitments made for political purposes in the campaign conditioned and controlled the foreign policies of the Eisenhower Administration, is all set forth with careful documentation in Professor Graebner's excellent book already mentioned. Its relevance here is that these relapses into the scapegoat simplification of complex and portentous problems are not merely the tolerable excesses of political stimulation; they carry a heavy price, too heavy in the light of present hazards.

I mention one more manifestation of the urge to simplify because, although it is well known, it is not always seen as a form of simplification. This is the kick-the-problem method. We all know that point of exasperation with baffling recalcitrance which makes us want to shake the child, kick the dog or the lawnmower. Rarely, however, do we reach the point achieved by an old soldier in our community who became so infuriated with his tractor that he got his shotgun and gave the machine both barrels. Sure enough, it started up all right, but it didn't go far. This mood of irritated frustration with complexity is not limited to the man in the street. It makes perhaps its most dangerous appearance among some pretty expert military planners as a result of the increasingly inescapable checkmate which nuclear retaliation poses to nuclear attack. The mental weariness induced finds expression in the suggestion, "Let's get it over with." That the "it" will in all probability be "us" does not seem to provide a conclusive reason against a course which is founded, not in reason, but in intellectual defeat and recourse to the demand for "simple answers to the most complex questions confronting human intelligence." [15] "Preventive war," a contradiction in terms, like the impulse to jump from dizzying

[15] The Honorable Dean Rusk, "The Conduct of Democracy's Foreign Policy," Address at Annual Dinner of the Canadian Society of New York, March 7, 1952, at New York.

heights, is the ultimate simplification, surrender to the urge toward self-destruction.

For Congress the problem of the future, as I see it, will be the increasing complexity of the tasks it will face and the increasing tendency to simplify the external world out of all semblance to the reality. If one seeks solutions to this dilemma, they are not likely to be found in formulas or in the mechanics of organization. Rather, the way to more effective legislative action is apt to lie through an honest and common-sense examination of how the dilemma arose.

A good way to begin might be to consider what, in the light of experience—some of which has been reviewed here—Congress can hope to do and what it cannot hope to do. It is pretty clear that it cannot hope to take over the executive task of administering the government. The temptation is well nigh irresistible. Partisan advantage and personal publicity are strong incentives. So the attempt will always be made and some damage will be done. For closely related reasons the Congress cannot, if the administration be weak, passive, or ineffective, drive it into vigorous action. There is no remedy for this situation save to live through it as best we may.

Similarly the formulation of policy, including as-
certaining, ordering, and appraising the facts upon
which it must be based, at our point in history, is
one requiring the central organization and direction
of great numbers of people and enterprises—which
the Congress cannot hope to perform.

All of this brings us back to an observation made
earlier in these pages, that time has brought about
a reversal of the legislative and executive roles as
conceived in the Constitution. Today—and even
more tomorrow—it is the President who initiates and
proposes policy; it is the Congress which approves,
modifies, or vetoes. This is a function which the
Congress can perform, legitimately descended from
the role of the representatives of the shires from the
earliest days—providing funds and manpower to
support policies of which they approved, and stal-
ling, when they did not approve, until some accept-
able compromise was reached.

With this orientation, the principal activity of
Congress today, investigation in all its branches—
the special committee with counsel, sleuths, publicity agents, radio and television, and the two hundred
or more standing committees, subcommittees and
joint committees charged with constant supervision
of the executive agencies—might take on a form

which could produce useful results. This would be as an aid to the debating of major policies—not trying to find out what are the plans, intentions, and the state of negotiations in the current flow of international business, but in making available the background of fact essential to any true appraisal of policy. It is not necessary to pry into secrets which would help our adversaries, but it is necessary continually to prod officialdom into letting our own people know what well-informed people elsewhere know.

With a firm and expanding foundation of solid fact, the Congress could really discuss many things. There has been no real discussion of foreign policy since the troops-for-Europe debate in the early months of 1951 (unless the Middle East discussion, which is in committee as I write, develops into one). It may not be irrelevant that Senator Vandenberg disappeared from the Senate at about the same time. The analysis and testing of policy by discussion—provided some broadly adequate basis of fact is available—is different from the making of policy. It is a part of it and an important part, a part which Congress could and most certainly should perform. Congress cannot initiate; it cannot create. But it can test and criticize and might well brand the mere-

tricious as such before it has had a chance to work
much harm.

. When Senators or Congressmen return from travel
and a half-hour interview with Khrushchev or Tito,
and then tell us definitely that the Russians do or do
not want peace, or that Tito is or is not sincere, they
are entering upon fields where they know little and
can find out less. The collection and appraisal of
intelligence is far more difficult and complicated
than they know. But a sustained and serious debate
on foreign policy in the committees and on the floor
by men who could take time to study and think
would perform a true congressional duty and could
bring clarification and focus to national judgment.
It could impose the penalty of scathing criticism
upon meretricious proposals and give support to
good ones. It could point out the way to think about,
appraise, and criticize policies.

How—to be concrete—can the non-expert member
of Congress go to work on problems of military
policy? First, by putting the tools of analysis to
work so that a point for discussion may stand out. I
have already touched upon how military policy
might be analyzed, but it will do no harm to repeat.

No American purpose, it could be pointed out,
depends upon our using force against anyone. But

we must be prepared to deter or meet the use of or the threat of force against our interests. When we speak of deterring the use of force against us, what do we mean? A deterrent is a threat under certain circumstances to do harm to another, which the other believes we will do and does not want to provoke. A threat is not believed, and therefore cannot deter, unless there is general conviction that the threatener has both the capacity and the intention to carry out the threat.[16]

The deterrent to the use or threat of nuclear bombs today is the belief by the initiator that he would receive retribution about as devastating as the attack. This deterrent will be effective to protect us only as long as it is believed elsewhere that we are maintaining the capacity and the will to launch a crushing nuclear reply if our vital interests are attacked.

But nuclear capacity will not deter all use of force against a nation possessing it, because it is not credible that many occasions are serious enough to lead that nation to use atomic weapons, and thereby incur the risk of having them used against it.

Atomic capacity did not save Dienbienphu or

[16] See William W. Kaufmann, "The Requirements of Deterrence," in *Military Policy and National Security* (Kaufmann, Ed., Princeton University Press, 1956), p. 12 *et seq.*

prevent Mr. Nasser from seizing the Suez Canal. It was not credible that it would be used.

Therefore, to deter or meet force used or threatened on a local basis, capacity in what are called conventional forces is required—that is, forces which can conduct limited warfare and keep it limited. Even these will not act as a deterrent or moderating factor unless others believe that they will be used. When the British Labour party and the United States Government pronounced against the use of force to counter the forceful seizure of the Suez Canal, Mr. Nasser could obviously no longer regard its use as a practical possibility.

This analysis—and similar analysis of political or economic policy in the foreign field—is susceptible of rational discussion by people who are not experts. With such modification as the discussion warranted, it could be adopted as a working hypothesis. In its light the Congress could examine a military program proposed by the President and draw conclusions helpful in performing its real duty of approving, modifying, or disapproving the program. If, for instance, it proved to be wholly lopsided, directed only toward atomic retaliation and omitting provision for capacity in conventional forces, and if a substantial need for forces of this kind were apparent in the light of the world situation, an issue could be sharply drawn and the bill could either be amended or rejected and returned to the executive with request for a more adequate program.

Or, if Congress had doubts as to the adequacy of the program in respect of deterring or meeting nuclear attack, it could turn its investigation and discussion, not to substituting its judgment for that of the executive branch in a technical field where Congress has no competence, but toward getting at and appraising the reasons for the inadequacy. To what extent, for instance, had what was necessary or desirable from a military point of view been subordinated to considerations of budgetary and fiscal policy? Was this necessary and wise? If not, and if further sums were available, how would the executive recommend that they be utilized as between nuclear offense and nuclear defense? In this way the Congress could make a real review and provide a real, as well as a useful, check and balance to executive impulses, the sources of which are not always apparent.

But to do this requires members of the House and Senate who have time to inform themselves and to think. It does not call for large staffs and extensive organization, but it cannot be done by men who spend the hours, when their chambers are not meeting, in going from one committee

meeting to another.[17] We all know the picture of
the busy legislator arriving breathless and late at
a committee meeting only to leave it early in order
to be late at the next one. And whatever time the
committees do not take is apt to be absorbed by the
demands of social life in Washington—the public
(official and unofficial) dinners and receptions by
diplomats, State societies, by the press, radio and
photographers, male and female, by famous host-
esses, and by the inevitable constituent and his wife
who have come to town. It is an interesting fact that
those members of the Washington community who
notoriously do their own thinking and their own
work—our judges—have the smallest staffs and lead
the most quiet lives.

Can the Congress discipline itself to do its own
job and not try to do the executive's job? Those who
know it best will have their doubts. The virus of
busyness has bitten deep. Impulses born of pa-

[17] "Committees," we are told by the London *Economist*, "it is
nowadays accepted, fall broadly into two categories, those
  "(A) from which the individual member has something to
  gain; and those
  "(B) to which the individual member has merely something
  to contribute.
"Examples of the B group, however, are relatively unimportant
for our purpose; indeed some people doubt whether they are
committees at all." "Parkinson Looks at Cabinet Governments,"
The Economist (London), Nov. 3, 1956, p. 395.

rochial interests at stake, of personal ambition, of partisan maneuver, all make for interference with administration and the attempt to control it. They are hard to resist in favor of more plain and unspectacular courses. But there have always been men in the Congress who have made this harder choice. Some, the present Speaker of the House, for instance, have the unquestioned respect of their colleagues. I doubt whether there are any mechanical aids to more mature, responsible, and restrained behavior. Clearly the restriction of time-consuming investigations to the essential minimum, and, in the Senate, a reduction in the size of the committees, with each Senator serving on only one committee, would help. But committee work will always be exacting. The task of concentration upon what members of a popular assembly can do amid the complexities of the twentieth century, and of doing that well, is a hard one. But I venture to say that upon the measure of its achievement will depend the future of representative government, the power of control exercised by a responsible legislature, in the United States.

Set in Linotype Caledonia
Format by Euclides P. Theoharides
Manufactured by The Haddon Craftsmen, Inc.
Published by HARPER & BROTHERS, *New York*